Lowell
Green

It's Hard to
Say Goodbye

Merry Christmas
Doris

Lowell Green

It's almost over…God, I've loved it!

Creative Bound International Inc.
www.creativebound.com

ISBN 978-1-894439-37-4
Printed and bound in Canada

Pre-press and production Creative Bound International Inc.

Library and Archives Canada Cataloguing in Publication

Green, Lowell, 1936-
    It's hard to say goodbye / Lowell Green.

Includes index.
ISBN 978-1-894439-37-4

    1. Green, Lowell, 1936-. 2. Radio talk shows—Ontario—Ottawa—History. 3. CFRA (Radio station : Ottawa, Ont.)—History. 4. Radio talk shows—Canada—History. 5. Radio broadcasters—Ontario—Ottawa—Biography. 6. Radio broadcasters—Canada—Biography. I. Title.
PN1991.4.G74A3 2007   791.44092   C2007-905469-2

This book is dedicated to the memory
of Harold Anthony Bitz,
known to legions of fans as Hal Anthony.
A great broadcaster and a great friend.

Happy days in the summer of 1994. Hal Anthony and
Gloria join Deborah and me atop a mountain in southern
France.

Contents

It's Hard to Say Goodbye

As the Good Book says, "to everything there is a season," and whether I care to admit it or not, my season as a broadcaster is just about over. The truth is, though, even after more than 50 years behind the microphone, it's awfully hard to say goodbye. It's kind of funny in a way. When I started in radio, my goal was to retire at the age of 45. I have no idea why I wanted to do that, because when I shut down "The Greenline" on July 1, 1978, at the age of 42, and moved on to other interests, I found I missed radio terribly.

I am certain I will miss it all terribly when I finally do pack it in for good, but right now the old bones are starting to complain bitterly about the 6:00 a.m. roll (sometimes fall) out of bed. And I've got to be honest with you; my brain isn't too crazy about those 40-below, pitch-black mornings with winds whipping snowdrifts across the Queensway!

Another thing that convinces me it's time to, at the very least, cut back drastically is the way the young pups in our newsroom look at me when I start pounding the desk and pulling my hair out at some gnat-brained bozo who wants to enlighten me on the proper methods of conducting talk shows! I'm not sure if the anxious looks from the newsroom derive from concern that I'm going to have the big one right there in the studio and have to be hauled out feet first, or disappointment that I might survive another idiot call and continue to occupy a coveted chair.

But you know what? No matter whether they haul me out feet first or I manage to hobble out under my own steam, it's been one wonderful ride. I wouldn't have missed a single moment of it, not even the nutcase callers. I've often thought that it was either Lady Luck smiling brightly or an angel was in my corner the day I walked into CKPC Radio in Brantford, Ontario, and started pounding out news stories on that battered old Remington. Come to think of it, Al Chandler, who first hired me, looked very much like a giant leprechaun!

Some of the characters I have met and write about here have gone on to great fame and fortune. Some are resting in that great studio in the sky. Others are probably in a drunk tank someplace. Several should, by rights, be locked up, and for all I know may be!

I've interviewed all our prime ministers since Lester Pearson (Jean Chrétien once campaigned for me!) and all Ottawa mayors since Ken Fogarty, but much more than that, in the past 50 years I have talked with more Canadians about more issues than any other person in the country. From the civil rights movement to gangsta rap, Diefenbaker to Harper, Vietnam to Afghanistan, I've argued and agreed, cried and laughed with countless numbers of tinkers and tailors, soldiers and sailors, leading citizens and crooks, doctors and druggies, wise men and nutbars, geniuses and fools...

God, I've loved it!

Goodbye Montreal;
Hello Ottawa

I'm standing amidst a small fortune of imported living room furniture trying not to look astonished as a $10,000 cheque bravely peeks out from a speeding boxcar and I'm asking myself what the heck I'm doing here.

Ten thousand dollars is all I'll likely earn in the next two years, and not only am I the only one in the room who thinks it's all pretty weird, but the 10-year-old birthday boy isn't the least bit interested, either in the cheque with his name on it or the electric train hauling it in a dizzying circle around and around the chesterfield. "Abandon all doubt, Lowell," I say to myself. "You are royally out of your league. Bailout time!"

It's summer 1960, four years since News Director Al Chandler took a chance on a 20-year-old kid fresh from shearing sheep and judging hogs at Macdonald Agricultural College and hired me as a legman (junior reporter) at CKPC Radio in Brantford. I've spent a year in the rocky wilds of Sudbury and Elliot Lake with CKSO-TV, suffered a few months at CKOX Radio in Woodstock, and been a year and a half in Montreal with United Press International and, more recently, DuPont Canada at their head office. I'm making decent money, but as I watch that $10,000 cheque making lazy circles around the living room, I realize that this is not only a world I do not understand, but one I do not wish to live in.

Diane is a very beautiful woman. A lovely woman. We have been discussing marriage, and as a possible future son-in-law her parents have invited me to their stately Montreal West home for the tenth birthday party of her little brother. The cheque—a thousand dollars for each year of the boy's life—is from his grandfather, one of Westmount's multi-millionaires. Diane comes from one of Montreal's wealthiest and most famous families.

As I look back on those days of such blissfully sweet ignorance and youthful promise, I don't think there is any shame in my admitting that I just couldn't handle the life which would surely settle around my shoulders if I married Diane. I am amazed that I had sufficient wits about me to recognize it. As much as I loved her, or thought I did, I just couldn't bring myself to plug into that kind of life.

Too far to travel, I suspect, for a kid who grew up on a farm where a dime was a small fortune, let alone ten thousand dollars.

It was there in that living room that I decided to end my love affair with Diane and with Montreal. I shed more than a few tears at the time, but I have never regretted the decision that eventually brought me to Ottawa.

But I have often wondered if I might have taken that giant leap into Diane's world, with my life taking a very different path, had I not arrived at that birthday party directly from an hour-long session with a priest, who for several weeks had been trying to convince me to convert to Catholicism. Was it the priest and the efforts to turn me into something I was not, or the toy boxcar sporting a $10,000 cheque that prodded me to say goodbye to Montreal and a life I was enjoying very much? Probably both. Don't get me wrong. The priest, as I recall, was a great guy, only following orders from Diane's grandfather, the major financial supporter of his church: "Turn that Protestant guy my granddaughter wants to marry into a Catholic."

Heaven only knows, I tried. So did the priest, but I think we both knew from the outset that while I might be able to fake a conversion for the sake of love, it would be a charade. I have never been a particularly religious person, but like so many of us raised by devout born-again Christians, Protestantism was so firmly embedded in my bones it could never truly be shaken free. The fact I didn't fake a conversion is probably an indication that neither Diane nor I were really ready to marry. I suspect that had it been the real thing, neither religion nor rich grandfathers would have deterred us.

Come to think of it, Diane didn't spend a whole lot of time grieving a lost love. It was only a few months after I fled the scene that she took that white-gowned stroll up the aisle on the arm of a broadly smiling grandfather. Judging from the very Irish name she acquired, I strongly suspect it was a proper Catholic they snagged!

Those were the days, of course, when things like religion and marriage actually mattered, especially when old Westmount money was involved.

I, on the other hand, lived more or less in a cave—a tiny one-room basement apartment not far from the Montreal West train station. One small window up-close-and-personal with a dusty sidewalk, one of those Canadian Tire canvas camp cots which I don't think they even sell anymore, an abandoned ironing board for a table, and that was pretty well it for interior decoration. Your typical bachelor pad at the turn of the decade. I suppose I must have had a fridge, although I don't recall ever having anything in it. As far as I know, the place didn't smell, although I recall some girls, upon entering, recoiling in some shock! In those days I really didn't notice things like that.

It was a little uncomfortable sitting there side by side on the camp cot with Diane's father one rainy night as he lectured me on the responsibilities I would be expected to shoulder if I married his daughter. "It wouldn't hurt," he said, as he finally rose to leave, his eyes darting around, "to get a couple of chairs in here."

Her grandfather, my address firmly in calfskin-gloved hand, set out one evening in his chauffeured limousine to track me down, but upon sighting rows of apartment buildings he became convinced they had taken a wrong turn. Believing they had entered a dangerous foreign ghetto, he ordered a hasty retreat to his mountain redoubt. Honestly, it was just as well.

As I look back today, I have no idea why I didn't have more furniture or more money for that matter. I was working at two jobs. DuPont Canada had hired me away from United Press International to take over as assistant editor of the company publication, *The Courier*, surely the most dreadfully tedious job on the face of the planet.

Unbeknownst to the suits at DuPont, I had been hired as a news anchor for CFCF-TV which had just been approved for Montreal by the Board of Broadcast Governors, but was not yet on the air. In fact, I was the first anchor thus hired, but while we waited for the miles of red tape to be sorted through, News Director Bert Cannings appointed me night news editor (6:00 p.m. till midnight) at CFCF Radio. (In another illustration of how small a world it is, Bert's son Richard Cannings later became an Ottawa city councillor.) Since in those days editors gathered and wrote the news and announcers only read (Bert disdainfully called the readers "golden throats"), DuPont had no way of knowing why I was dragging my butt around so much during the day!

Not that dragging your butt made much difference with that job. It's a wonder my brain survived the stupefying, crushing boredom of helping to turn out a six-page publication once a month. Much of my time was engaged in getting written approval from hordes of plant and office managers for features that usually weren't much more than a five-line story about an employee at some plant scoring 20 points against a local high school basketball pickup team. My greatest journalistic achievement with DuPont was to compose a caption for a staged safety promotion photo of somebody pretending to fall down a set of stairs.

Just as every hockey player remembers his first NHL goal, almost 50 years later I still remember, word for word, the caption that earned me my first "Office Memo of Merit." Believe it or not, this is the magnificent gem I struggled with for days and finally, in a burst of creativity, gave painful birth to: "This worker will doubtless make it to the bottom, but upon which end will he land?" Great stuff, eh? They actually paid me $90 a week for this kind of blinding brilliance!

The editor of *The Courier* was a little sandy-haired Scotsman named Denny Oglivie who, after my creation of the award-winning caption, informed me in a moment of collegial confidentiality that the company had great hopes for me. This came as a great shock to me since I certainly didn't have great hopes for the company and, in particular, my continued efforts on its behalf.

Denny constantly sported one of those very expensive meerschaum pipes he called Alice, and in moments of high creativity he would light up old Alice, place his feet firmly on his desk and nod off. "ICC—intense creative contemplation," he explained. It was in this state of ICC that he first drew my attention to the woman who was eventually to drive me from DuPont, CFCF and Montreal.

Either Denny had the ability to see through his lids, or on this occasion his eyes were not fully closed, because his feet suddenly shot off his desk with a whomp to the floor, and Alice was ripped from his lips. "My God," he exclaimed with a gasp, "those are magnificent breasts!"

This isn't a Harlequin Romance or any kind of bodice-ripper so I won't go into any kind of soliloquy about liquid almond eyes, a languid walk or enchanting laugh, other than to say that Denny Ogilvie's observation as Diane strolled by our office was absolutely correct. I do wish to confirm that the magnificence extended far beyond that which Denny very correctly identified. She was a beauty! And so, thus alerted, the universal chase was on, with me in panting pursuit. And that's before I knew she was rich!

What beauty and testosterone hath drawn together shall money and religion cast asunder! Little did I know that my few months of boredom at DuPont would also, in the end, play a major role in bringing me to Ottawa, and may even have played a role in the birth of the Montreal Expos! (*See "The Expos and Me," page 106.*)

The Great Escape

Three years previously, I jammed everything I owned into a 1956 Meteor and headed north up Highway 11 from CKPC Brantford to Sudbury and a year of high adventure with CKSO-TV. Now I am heading up Highway 17 west from Montreal to Ottawa, which I have been warned is not only a city bereft of adventure, but good-looking women as well. Perfect! I've had enough good-looking women for awhile, to say nothing of mind-numbing jobs and rich grandfathers.

I realize as I clear the outskirts of Montreal West that I'm not making particularly good progress down the highway of life, since this time I'm able to loosely pack everything I own (minus camp cot and ironing board) into a two-seat MG, no jamming required! I console myself with the knowledge that while I owe as much to the bank for the MG as I did for the '56 Meteor when I headed for the frozen north three years ago, at least this is a 1960 model, almost brand new. And, best of all, tucked firmly in my back pocket is a job offer. Chief News Editor at CFRA in Ottawa, which, let's face it, is a considerable upgrade from Sudbury!

"We await your arrival with great excitement," says the note from CFRA News Director Campbell McDonald. Since no one had ever awaited my arrival with even minimal excitement, I am very impressed. Little do I know that Campbell spends a fair amount of time in a state of excitement. Gord Atkinson, who was at CFRA the day I arrived, claims that when I pulled up in front of the station in my little MG, Campbell hustled everyone to the window and said with great excitement, "Here comes Lorne Green!" (I swear this is true.)

The goodbye back in Montreal West with Diane had been one of those tawdry, teary scenes Hollywood loves so much, but in truth I think we were both more than a little relieved the drama was finally over. While I never heard, I suspect her grandfather wasn't too badly broken up about it and I'm sure the friendly little priest was reassured there really is a God! Strangely enough, Diane's father did seem a little disappointed. Despite my obvious lack of home-decorating skills, I think he saw something in me that I didn't discover in myself for several years.

I remember as though it was yesterday, her father, a tall grey-faced man who always seemed to walk around in a fog of semi-puzzlement over the wealth into which he had been born, taking me aside one day with obvious serious intent. "Oh, oh," I said to myself, "what's up now? Has old Granddaddy laid down the law?" To tell the truth, at that point, I was kind of hoping he might try a hefty "get lost" bribe, which—depending upon its heftiness—I might be prepared to accept.

But it had nothing to do with Diane. He sat me down on the chesterfield around which would spin the toy train and its $10,000 burden a few weeks later. "I was listening to CJAD this morning," he said rather shyly, obviously hoping I wouldn't be offended by his disloyalty to CFCF. I stared at him blankly. "I didn't catch his name, but there's this guy reading some kind of editorial giving hell to Montreal drivers. It was really good—interesting." He waited for some reaction, but I had no idea where he was going with this and said nothing. "You know," he continued, "maybe that's the kind of thing you should look into…seems to me there might be more money in opinion than news."

I was so all garbled up with his daughter, Catholic priests, photo captions and overdue car payments that I didn't pay much attention at the time. Was a seed planted?

Golden Throats

If it was a lost love's father who planted the opinion seed, it was probably Bert Cannings who delayed its sprouting. CFCF's News Director back in Montreal hated announcers with a passion. Something you have to agree is mighty strange for a guy whose chosen profession surrounds him with the objects of his discontent. "Golden throats," he called them, with obvious disdain. The CFCF newsroom had a caste system as entrenched as anything in India. As news gatherers and writers, we were encouraged to not even talk to those who read the news and never ever to write anything on the page which we did not intend to be read.

My father used to tell the story about a little cockney sergeant who greeted each new raw recruit to boot camp in Texas with horror stories about sex. Grave warnings about appendages swelling up and falling off, brains being littered with holes. You get the picture. His lectures were always concluded with a wonderful little homily—"and remember this, me buys, there's lots of duh-tay gulls for duh-tay buys!" After which, back in barracks, the men would shout in unison, "There's lots of duh-tay gulls for duh-tay buys—SO LET'S GO GET 'EM!!"

With Bert Cannings the warnings were about "golden throats." His horror story was about a former announcer at CFCF (or so he claimed) who was so dumb he read on air a brief note the editor had penned as a joke at the end of the story. "Go f—- yourself." Today, something like that or even worse would hardly raise a ripple, it's become so commonplace on radio and television, but in the late 1950s that word making it to air was every announcer's worst nightmare.

As Bert told the story, his beefy red face would puff up even more, his tangled eyebrows rippling up and down his face like Pacific waves on a stormy day.

"We hired you, because you are a writer," he told me, "so write; stay away from the golden throats. Fortunately, they're too dumb to be dangerous, but don't waste your time. Don't even talk with them." And finally this admonition: "Don't write a thing on the page you don't want them to read. I even had one guy so dumb he read the '30' someone wrote at the end of the story."

I didn't doubt him for a moment. I had disgraced myself a couple of years ago in a sorry attempt at announcing at CKOX Woodstock when, as I read a commercial for a local drive-in-theatre movie entitled *Attack of the Crab Monsters*, I made the mistake of glancing up to see my producer apparently ripping his crotch to shreds. My resultant performance (bouts of hysterical laughter interspersed with a few lines of news) had convinced me my path to fame and fortune was as far removed from a live microphone as possible.

Bert Cannings may have been a bit loopy about announcers, but there was surely no one in the country who knew more about how radio news should be written. When I started at CKPC in Brantford, audience attention spans were obviously a considerable bit longer than they are today. Newscasts would regularly last 15 minutes—more news than you are likely to hear on many big city music radio stations in an entire day today. Individual stories would sometimes ramble on for minutes. There were even fewer time constraints at CKSO-TV in Sudbury where we had to fill hour-long newscasts. I once produced a dandy little feature on a farmer who scrubbed his turnips in his wife's washing machine. The story was even nominated for some kind of award, which proves, if nothing else, that TV was just as bad back then as it is today!

As Features Editor of United Press International, my copy was never edited, so when I landed at CFCF I desperately needed the Bert Cannings crash course in radio writing.

No story longer than six lines. "First line's got to grab the listener by the #@#!!" (What female listeners were supposed to grab wasn't made clear, nor did we dare ask!). "I don't give a sweet damn if the world is to come to an end in the next half hour—six lines are all it gets. If you can't write it in six lines, get a job as a baker." Long pause. "Or as a #@# golden throat!" Bert Cannings' messages didn't take six lines!

Bert wasn't entirely from the old school, however. He believed in the carrot as well as the stick. At the start of each shift every one of us would rush to the filing cabinet and pull out the stories we had written the day before. What we were looking for was a red-circled lead sentence on one of our carefully crafted stories. A red circle meant we had gained favour with Bert and, thus, had won a red lollipop! No, I'm not kidding. Forget the red badge of courage, at CFCF a red circle meant you had composed a lead sentence that in Bert Cannings' judgement had grabbed the audience you know where and you were thus empowered to open the large cigar box on the corner of his desk, remove a red lollipop and suck it as noisily as possible.

I won my share of lollipops, but the only winning sentence I can recall referred to Lester Pearson who was in the midst of a seven-nation European visit. I don't recall exactly what I wrote—something about Pearson donning seven-league boots to take giant strides across Europe. Nobody, including the guy who read the story on air, had the faintest idea what seven-league boots were, but Bert claimed he believed in fairy tales and thought it was lollipop good!

Bert Cannings was named to the Canadian Media Hall of Fame in 1986, and in 1994, a year after his death, he was inducted into the Association of Broadcasters' Hall of Fame. He served several terms as president of the Radio and Television News Directors Association and was the winner of countless awards during his 55-year career in broadcasting. Interestingly enough, since I arrived in Ottawa, the CFRA News Department has won several awards established in Bert Cannings' name.

Despite the brief time I spent under his tutelage, Bert played a major role in my career, and there have been more than a few occasions as I am about to turn my microphone on for another three hours of talk when I wonder if even as a "golden throat" he might still have a lollipop or two for me in that old cigar box.

Bert Cannings was one of those wonderful characters the wild and woolly early days of broadcasting used to attract, but if you wanted to find a guy who was really out there on the edge you had to head north to a moonscape of barren rocks and find the man who in 1957 hired me away from CKPC in Brantford to CKSO-TV in Sudbury.

Wild Man Wilf

I've made it back through a fierce blizzard to my hovel at the base of the CKSO-TV transmitter in Elliot Lake when I get the news: "Wilf has fired you!" The bearer of these glad tidings is the switchboard operator back at base camp CKSO-TV head office and studios in Sudbury. I'm incredulous. "Fired me?! What are you talking about, fired me? Who fired me? Why? Let me talk to the newsroom. I've got a major story here. A stupid snowplow driver has just taken out the bridge at Blind River; the Trans-Canada Highway is totally shut down. We've got cars piled up for miles in both directions. Put me through to the newsroom." There's something that sounds almost like a sob. "There's nobody in the newsroom! Wilf fired them, too!" She lets out a long sigh. "I'm the only one here."

I'm thinking this is crazy. This woman must have been sniffing one of the INCO smokestacks or something.

I finally get the story.

It's late December. Christmas parties are in the air. I missed the big one last night at Danny Kelley's apartment, thanks to being stuck up here in the most godforsaken place on earth in winter. The party got a little rowdy and then some joker pulled out a tape recorder and started asking various celebrants stupid questions—the most stupid of which was, "So, what do you think of Wild Man Wilf?"

Since Wild Man Wilf is Wilf Woodill, General Manager of CKSO Radio and Television and reputed to be half-nuts, you can just imagine what that old tape recorder taped. Unprintable, believe me!

I suppose every organization has its spies or as we used to call them brown-nosers, so as you might imagine, it doesn't take long for the tape to end up on the Wild Man's desk.

Since I wasn't there, the rest of what I tell you is part myth, part speculation, part truth.

"Who was at the party?" screams the Wild Man. "Everyone," lies the squealer.

"Then tell them all they are fired," yells the Wild Man. "Everyone?"

gulps the squealer. "Everyone except you and make sure we've got someone on the switchboard, so when the ungrateful bastards phone in to complain I can let them have a piece of my mind and not a cent of severance for anyone!"

Not since its launch on October 25, 1953, as Canada's first private television station have Sudbury viewers of CKSO-TV seen anything like it. Almost an hour of a year-old church service, interrupted twice by long bouts of static, interrupted by brief flashes of the test pattern; last night's newscast is repeated several times. So many calls of complaint and concern flood the switchboard that the poor woman finally pulls the plug and fires herself!

The craziness doesn't end until late afternoon with the Kay Woodill Show. As Wild Man Wilf's wife, Kay has special status and has thus been spared the mass firing. On the set for her fashion show, Kay becomes extremely agitated when she spots Wilf behind the camera and the squealer trying to man the lights. "I can't do a show like this," she complains. "Wilf, you don't know anything about camera work. Where's the soundman?" To which I have it on excellent authority, Wilf replies. "Oh hell, just talk loud!"

Finally, with his wife threatening to walk off the set and for all I know out of his life, the Wild Man turns to the squealer and says, "Where is everybody?" "You fired them, Wilf!" "Well," growls the Wild Man, "you get on the phone and tell everybody if they don't get back here right now, I'll fire the whole damn lot of them again!"

It is the only time since starting in radio in 1956 that I have ever been unemployed.

Although I came mighty close to it again a few months later. I am on Manitoulin Island filming a feature on a fish hatchery when a truck rams a pole and the entire island is blacked out. No hydro, and no phones either, since the phones in those days went through an operator-manned switchboard. (No cellphones in those days!) To make matters worse, the old swing bridge onto the island is jammed in the open position. We're trapped for the better part of 12 hours.

Thus it is that I have no way of knowing that Wild Man Wilf is beside himself. He's heard that the island has been blacked out, a major story, but where the heck is his star reporter Green, the lazy, no-good bum? When the phones are finally back in operation, I call our news anchor Bill Kehoe (yes, the same Bill Kehoe who "golden throated" for so many years with CBC Ottawa) to bring him up-to-date. "Geez," he whispers, "Wilf's here, mad as hell, says he's been trying to find you for hours." Before I get a chance to catch my breath, the Wild Man is on the phone. "Where have you been?" he's yelling at the top of his voice. "Half of northern Ontario is without power for most of the day, the place is going crazy and you're off sleeping some damn place!" I try to explain what happened. "Wilf, there was nothing I could do—the power was out—the phones were out—the bridge was out. What could I do? I had no way of getting in touch with the station, let alone file a story."

This, I swear on a stack of bibles, is truly, word for word, what the Wild Man replies: "HAVEN'T YOU EVER HEARD OF PIGEONS?!" And he hangs up.

I never talked with Wilf again, but since employment security didn't appear to be job one in Sudbury, when CKOX in Woodstock offered me a job as news director, sports director, farm director and chief announcer (possibly the only announcer), I headed south for the big time!

No Peace and Love at This Woodstock

Forget that song about herding cows, you don't know what lonely is till you get to work in Woodstock! CKOX masquerading as radio in Woodstock, Ontario, that is. I don't know what that little town is like today, but in 1958 it was the armpit of Ontario, maybe the entire country. At least, as far as I was concerned. Forget your small-town friendliness; here was a place about as cold, insular and bigoted toward newcomers as you were likely to find in the deepest south in those days. A town, believe me, that richly deserved the terrible radio programming provided by my employer.

Sudbury and Elliot Lake, as raw and dangerous as they were, opened their arms to strangers of all races and nationalities. Drop into any pub, any night, in either town, and the place would be loudly abuzz, sometimes raucous with five or six languages pounding away at your senses. I never did find a pub in Woodstock. If you did you can be certain it wouldn't be abuzz with anything, and I suspect the sound of a foreign language would have prompted a hushed silence followed by a mass exodus.

My experience in Brantford, Sudbury and Elliot Lake was that those of us in broadcasting formed a kind of fraternity that made establishing friendships quick and easy. Indicate any degree of friendliness and within days you'd be invited out for a couple of drinks, or over to someone's house to watch a hockey game or, upon occasion, to provide a shoulder to cry on.

No chance of that in Woodstock. The closest I came to establishing any kind of relationship at CKOX was with Peter Rabbits, our chief engineer whose crotch ripping while I was reading an advertisement for the movie entitled *Attack of the Crab Monsters* almost ended my career as a broadcaster.

It wasn't until my six months in Woodstock purgatory was almost over that I discovered the main reason for my being ostracized. I had managed to convince a pretty little blond to go out on a couple of dates. A movie and an A & W drive-in was pretty well the extent of it, as I recall. But when I came calling the third time, it was an immediate strikeout. I'll never forget it. There was accusation in her voice on the phone: "My parents say I can't go out with you." I was more than a little puzzled. We'd had fun on the dates. She was living at home, but she was my age, 22, for heaven's sake. I reminded her of this, and then naturally asked what the heck was up with her parents, whom I had never met. There was a tiny hesitation in her voice when she hit me with this: "You're Jewish and my parents don't want me dating a Jew. You should have told me!" I was so totally caught off guard, it was so outrageous, that I burst out laughing. At which point she hung up on me and I never talked with her again.

A few lights began to go off in my head, so the next morning I walked into the sales office at CKOX and accosted the first person I met, the elderly secretary who had studiously avoided me from the day I walked in. "Hey," I said, "do you think I'm Jewish? Is that why you won't give me the time of day around here?" She didn't appear the least bit flustered, which had certainly been my intent. "I have no idea what you are talking about, Mr. Green," she said. "I am not prejudiced against Jews. I'm sure you are all very nice people!"

I left my resignation on station owner Monty Wherry's desk, but it wasn't until I went back to the little room over a garage I was living in and started packing that my anger changed to laughter. I can't say I laughed until the tears came, but even today I can see the wry humour in it.

During my first year at Macdonald College in 1954, I carried on a torrid love affair with a lovely Jewish girl named Patsy Guttman. I had even been invited to the Guttman home on Victoria Avenue in Westmount and had been treated with great respect. But when the relationship became serious it was quickly cut off by those very same parents who didn't want to take the chance their daughter would marry a Christian. Now, in Woodstock, because my last name is Green and I'm in radio, I'm ostracized and a relationship is severed because they think I'm Jewish!

Please remember this was only about 12 years after we discovered the extent of the Holocaust!

I couldn't wait to get out of that place and head for Montreal, completely unaware, of course, that in another year or so I'd be in a grand-parental doghouse for not having the good sense to be Catholic!

News on the Cheap

I'll say this about working for United Press International (UPI), they couldn't have cared less about your religion. As long as you were talented and cheap—very, very cheap—they loved you.

I started at CKPC in Brantford for $60 a week plus the odd bowl of free soup if you worked all night. I was rolling in riches in Sudbury with a salary of $100 a week. At Woodstock it was back down to $60 which is what they're paying me to be Features Editor here at UPI, so I'm not exactly making good progress.

When I arrived in late summer 1958, having just escaped Woodstock, UPI had just launched a Canadian wire service for radio.

I have no idea how they managed to finance this, since the company was chronically short of funds. The joke (or at least we hoped it was a joke) in the huge, steamy barn-like newsroom was that only the fleetest of foot could make it to the bank in time to get their paycheques cashed.

My job was to review all the news flooding into our Montreal office from such news wires as AP and Reuters, as well as from our own reporters in the field around the world, and rewrite the major stories for the more than 100 radio stations across the country receiving our service.

The workload was incredible. Each hour I had to gather, edit and write two sets of reports. One we called WIBS which stood for "World in Brief"—designed for a five-minute newscast, followed by a "World"—essentially the same stories but with more details, designed for a 10- or 15-minute newscast. All of this I punched onto a giant master keyboard that made a terrible racket.

Thank heavens I had grown up milking cows or my fingers, I swear, would have been crippled from the effort of pounding that infernal keyboard. After a while you learned to get the thing going in a kind of syncopated rhythm that would literally shake the floor. We were located on the second floor of an ancient building on Beaver Hall Hill near St-Jacques, which if not condemned as unsafe, unsightly and unsanitary, should have been! Sweat shops were supposed to have been abolished by that time, but with no air conditioning, windows so rusted they could not be opened and with dozens of hot, clanking Teletype machines, it would have put anything in rural China to shame, I am sure.

In the unlikely event that I had any spare time, I was supposed to assist in editing news for our newspaper division. In part, this was similar to what I was doing on the radio side—gathering and editing news from around the world—only this time for Canadian newspapers.

There was one major difference here, however. There was no way anyone would have the time to gather news from sources around the world and retype it for distribution to our newspaper subscribers. It would take a small army of typists to meet the demands of the dozens of newspapers using our service, especially in light of the different time zones that meant different deadlines. In addition, many newspapers in those days had afternoon editions as well as morning ones.

Thus, attached to every incoming news wire was a little gizmo that typed the words in code, resembling a kind of reverse Braille. Instead of raised dots representing each letter of the Braille alphabet, our code was a series of holes in a paper tape. You were supposed to be able to read the code, edit it for length, slice the tape in the appropriate place with a razor blade, and then place the coded tape into a machine that would then transmit written copy to Teletype printers in newspaper offices across the country. If we didn't have the coded tape, it meant that we would have to manually type the story and retransmit it to our subscribers.

The day I arrived, News Editor Tommy McQuaid gave me a handful of coded tapes and a code book. "Take these home this weekend, study them and be ready to read them on Monday," he instructed.

Fat chance of that! I don't think I could have decoded those tapes in a year. All I did was figure out which series of holes represented a period at the end of a sentence. Depending upon the amount of news on the day's run, I would simply count the sentences and cut the tape at what I considered a sufficient number of sentences. On a heavy run day, I might let a story go ten sentences—on a slow day, maybe fifteen.

The scheme worked perfectly. I became noted for my ability to keep international news concise.

The fact that I was also Features Editor, but really had few features to write, meant that I was expected to be available for other spur-of-the-moment assignments. Generally this meant when Sports Editor

Dick Bacon didn't feel like covering something himself, he sent the only guy who didn't refuse, which was me.

I hadn't been there more than a week when he sent me off to McGill Stadium to cover an exhibition game between the Montreal Alouettes and the Edmonton Eskimos. I had absolutely no idea how to do this. The only players I could identify were Sam (The Rifle) Echeverry for Montreal and Normie Kwong for Edmonton. The press box was a rickety wooden shed attached precariously high atop the south stands. (I would imagine it has been considerably improved today!)

What I didn't know, because no one told me, was that as play progressed I was supposed to dictate the storyline to a Teletype operator who shared the tiny booth with me. If all went according to the plan, of which I had no knowledge, at the conclusion of the game, all I would have to do was write the lead paragraph and the story was done.

If I could find that Teletype operator today, so help me, I would give him a big kiss. He saved my hide. Seeing that I had no idea what to do, he began to write the story himself, punching out what turned out to be pretty good copy as the game progressed.

When I got back to the newsroom after the game, I found that the only thing that had been rewritten before being fired off to newspapers across the county was my only contribution, the lead paragraph! "Not punchy enough," said Mr. Bacon. But wonder of wonders, despite the fact that I had contributed absolutely nothing but a pile of worry to the story, there right under the really punchy headline "The Rifle Shoots Down the Eskimos" were the glorious words, *By Lowell Green*. My first byline! Better than money! Well, almost!

Either I hadn't screwed up too badly or they were scraping the bottom of the barrel again, because a few weeks later Dick Bacon gave me my first really big break at UPI. "I've got two assignments for you, Green," he said. "First, interview Yvon Durelle prior to his light heavyweight championship fight with Archie Moore in the Montreal Forum, and then after the fight get into the winner's dressing room and give us a good colour story."

It was a terrific fight. Front page coverage around the world. But featured on almost as many sports pages as the fight itself was the story I wrote about Durelle, down on his hands and knees playing craps with his trainers minutes before the biggest fight of his life. Almost as widely read was the little story I wrote from Archie Moore's dressing room after his victory about a pugnacious woman photographer with the build of a fire hydrant, who reduced us all (including a badly bloodied Moore) to riotous laughter when she threatened to come down off her chair and "kick the shit" out of Archie Moore if he didn't smile for her camera.

It was only a few weeks after the fight that my stories of the Springhill Mine disaster were on the front pages of newspapers around the world, DuPont offered me a job as assistant editor of their company publication, and Diane entered my life.

Finally, I'm Live

"If you want me as a guest on your show tomorrow, lad, you'll have to come down here to the farm to pick me up," says my father. I grump about the two-hour drive from Ottawa to Ormstown, Quebec, but agree. Thank goodness, because shortly after arriving I go back to the creek behind his farmhouse to find out what the yelling is all about, and there is my father, pinned up against the tractor by Old Mildred, a thousand pounds or so of very angry black Galloway cow. He's half laughing, half crying, but you can tell he's in no little pain. "Jumpin' geez, lad, where have you been? I've been yelling my head off for half an hour. Get her off me before she breaks every bone in my body!"

This is easier said than done. Old Mildred is dripping with mud from her belly down, her legs are quivering with anger and fatigue, but she's got her head firmly planted in my father's chest leaning heavily into him and every once in while she gives him a little snort and a bunt which starts him yelling again. To complicate matters, a rope fastened to the tractor hitch and looped around the cow's front quarters has become entangled so that my father, Old Mildred and the tractor are firmly trussed together. If Galloway cows had horns, my father would have stopped yelling some time ago.

"Ungrateful damn cow," he grunts through clenched teeth. "She's so stupid she gets stuck in the ditch, I pull her out with the tractor and this is the thanks I get!" He starts to laugh, but the pain cuts it off. "Geez, I think she's broken a couple of my ribs." He starts to swear a blue streak as Old Mildred bucks up a bit of energy and gives him another good whack with her head.

This is not the first instance of my father's kindness toward the multitude of animals and fowl that crowd his farm near Ormstown, backfiring on him. Only the week previously, a calf nudged up against the bottom of a ladder propped up against the barn. Unfortunately, my father happened to be perched on top of the ladder nailing a loose board. The calf was one he had rescued from a disinterested mother. My father and his new wife, Cheryl, had fed it with a baby bottle until the calf, unable to distinguish between baby bottle and cow's udder, followed them around like—well, a pet calf. Dislodging the base of the ladder, as far as the calf was concerned, was just a way of saying I love you.

Thankfully, the fall wasn't far and into a manure pile so the damage was mainly to pride and not body.

This time, however, the body isn't so fortunate. It is mayhem not love that Old Mildred has in mind. I finally manage to get tractor, cow and father unhitched without further damage. Once released from the rope, Old Mildred turns and glares crazy-eyed at me for a moment, but figures, I suppose, she'd done enough damage for one day and hobbles off toward the herd.

Thus it was that the next day my father's laughter, as he joins me on my first bona fide live broadcast on CFRA in Ottawa, is somewhat constrained by two cracked ribs.

I say bona fide since, in truth, I had done some "on the spot" reporting from fires and accidents, but it is early June 1962 when Frank Ryan first entrusts me to cover off for him on some of his famous "Farmer's Notebook" segments and my career as a "golden throat" is truly launched. Those of you who have been around the Ottawa Valley for any length of time know that the late Frank Ryan, founder of CFRA, had become a legend by the 1960s. Rumour had it that even barnyard animals stopped what they were doing at 12:15 p.m. each day at the sound of the show's "Surrey With the Fringe on Top" theme song and Frank's heavily Ottawa Valley-accented opening line, "Hello Folks!"

With the Woodstock disaster firmly in mind, I decide to invite my father onto the show as a special guest. A veteran at the microphone, he'll cover off for me if I stop breathing or get a serious brain cramp! I'm only too well aware that if I goof up this time I may never get another chance at a live microphone.

I need not have worried. It was nerve-racking, and Frank Ryan had mighty big shoes to fill, but some 40 years later I still have people coming up to me saying, "Do you remember the time you told the story about rescuing your dad from that crazy cow? Lowell, I never laughed so hard in all my life!"

Old Mildred has long since departed for that great green pasture in the sky. My father and I shared many more adventures before he succumbed to leukemia, but every once in a while I think back and realize that it was on that bright June day in that tiny studio at 150 Isabella Street, with my father wincing in pain at every laugh, that I began to wonder if perhaps there was a career for me as a "golden throat."

Passing Through

I know, I know. Telling stories about dumb Americans is just looking for a cheap joke and I discourage it whenever possible. Let's face it, we've got a few homegrowns who aren't all that swift either. (Listen to my show sometime!) But I've got to tell you about the first time I ever spoke into a microphone.

The year is 1956. I've only just begun at CKPC in Brantford. I'm as green as grass, not exactly sure what a radio station even does, but our News Director, Al Chandler, sends me out with a tape recorder to interview some tourists. "Time to get your feet wet," he says.

It's for a Saturday afternoon program called "Welcome to Brantford." The idea is to interview a few tourists passing through town and, if possible, get them to say something nice about Canada—or maybe if they are confused enough and you get really lucky, you might even find someone prepared to say something nice about Brantford!

I am literally shaking with fear as I stand there on downtown Colborne Street looking for a "victim." "Nothing to it," snorts Al, who has never been near a microphone in his life and has no intentions of doing so. "You just find some turkey with a Yankee licence plate, stick the mic in his face, turn on this switch on and ask some questions." Yeah right, Al, nothing to it indeed!

And then I spot him. Your typical American tourist: big, friendly looking, stogie poked in his face, wearing some kind of pink and yellow shorts no self-respecting Brantfordian would be caught dead in. Little did I realize that the following exchange, word for word, would be the first time my voice was broadcast on radio. Unfortunately (fortunately?), no one remembers what I said.

Closing my eyes, with courage cranked up, I step forward with microphone and tape recorder. "Welcome to Brantford."

He turns with a big smile. "Why, thank you. What's this for?" He points to the mic. I explain. He's magnanimous. "I love this country. Been across it at least a dozen times!"

Now he's got me. "You've flown across Canada a dozen times?" He rolls the cigar into the side of his mouth. "No, sir. I drive across!"

I'm incredulous, all fear evaporates. "You've driven across Canada a dozen times! I've got to tell you, most Canadians have never driven across the country even once. It must have taken you months."

He looks at me strangely. "No, sir, I can do it in a day. It's not that hard!"

I've still got that recording. You can hear the disbelief in my voice. "You drive across Canada in a day?! What are you driving?"

"This here old buggy," he says, pointing to a '54 Ford Fairlane with Michigan plates. "We come in at Windsor and go out at Niagara Falls—no problem at all doing her in a day!"

You don't hear my reply…only about two minutes of canned laughter the producer dubbed in. What a way to launch a career!

Up, Up and Away!

It's the scorpions that have me worried. And the snakes. I've been warned about both. "Especially dangerous at night," according to our shuttle bus driver. "Wouldn't catch me out there in that desert after sundown for all the tea in China," he announces. "Damn things are so vicious they'll jump right up and grab you by the throat!" So here I am, so far past sundown it's getting close to midnight, and not only am I in the desert, I'm lying on my belly smack dab in the middle of it. It would be ridiculously easy for anything to grab my throat.

I don't know it at the time, but I am about to make history.

In less than one minute, I will go to air from the California desert with the only live broadcast of what has been deemed to be one of the ten most outstanding achievements in the first 100 years of engineering in Canada.

It actually began almost five years earlier on October 4, 1957, with an eerie BEEP, BEEP, BEEP while millions of earthlings gazed skyward in hopes of catching a glimpse of a tiny moving light that was SPUTNIK!

Remember that? Remember where you were? That's the day the Space Age is launched, with the Soviets in the lead during the height of the Cold War.

Embarrassed and more than a little frightened at the ramifications, the Americans launch their first satellite, Explorer 1, on January 31, 1958, after which they solicit proposals for the involvement of scientists from other countries in joint space programs. Canada responds quickly.

Those of us who lived through that period know how real the threat of nuclear war was. MAD (mutually assured destruction) was everyone's nightmare. We built backyard bomb shelters, air-raid sirens sprouted on many streets, and our children were taught to duck beneath their desks to avoid the blast. Between 1959 and 1961, the Diefenbunker, known officially as the Central Emergency Government Headquarters, was built in Carp. The four-storey-deep bunker, named after then Prime Minister John Diefenbaker, was designed to withstand a significant nuclear blast and serve as the site for government to continue to function in some fashion after an attack.

At the Defence Research Bureau (DRB) in Ottawa, scientists were especially concerned with our ability to communicate in the far north. This was where the Distant Early Warning network of radar stations, known as the DEW Line, was established to detect incoming Soviet missiles in time for us to seek shelter and launch retaliatory nuclear warheads. High frequency (HF) radio was the primary means of communication prior to satellites, but HF radio depends on reflections from the ionosphere. Particularly in the north, due to interference from the northern lights, this could be very unreliable.

Research underway at the Defence Research Telecommunications Establishment (DRTE) was directed primarily at trying to improve communications via various radio bands, but the scientists were severely hampered by a scarcity of ionospheric data. All they could study were the lower layers. Scientists had long dreamed of using a satellite to study the ionosphere from above. Whether any scientists at that time even dreamed that the satellites themselves could be used for communications is unclear.

So it was that when the Americans came knocking, asking for space proposals, we threw the door wide open. We offered to build a satellite that would place an ionospheric sounder in orbit and, in April 1959, signed an agreement with NASA whereby Canada would supply the satellite and NASA would launch it.

Thus, on September 29, 1962, Alouette 1 is perched atop a mighty Thor Agena B rocket ready for launch from the desert of Vandenberg Air Force Base in California and I'm a few hundred feet away lying on my stomach trying to hook a primitive microphone to a telephone in preparation for a live broadcast of the historic blast-off. CFRA listeners back in Ottawa wait breathlessly. (Actually, hundreds of those who had worked for a year or more on Alouette did stay up all night to listen. You can imagine their anticipation!)

Today, of course, broadcasting live from any place in the world is a simple matter—thanks to one of hundreds of satellites circling the globe. But in 1962, the best means of long-distance communication was through land lines—in other words, the telephone. To accommodate me and the CBC's Knowlton Nash, who also planned a live broadcast, someone had hauled a small bank of telephones mounted on a wagon-like contraption to the media viewing site (a pile of sand!).

My plan was that as the countdown reached 30 seconds before launch, I would alert CFRA, then unscrew the mouthpiece of the telephone and clip two wires leading from the bulky microphone I had lugged from Ottawa, to two wires inside the mouthpiece of the phone. Like a soldier before entering battle, I had practised this delicate manoeuvre until I could do it with my eyes closed. Which is a mighty good thing because the one thing the scientists running the outfit had forgotten was lights; we were in total darkness out there in the barren desert, and the noise was so loud the only way I could hear anything back at CFRA was to crawl under the wagon. All of this, mind you, had to be done in 30 seconds with the image of scorpions, snakes and goodness knows what dancing in my head.

As the broadcast, now resting in the National Archives, proves, I performed the feat in 25 seconds, giving listeners to CFRA (at about 3:00 a.m. Ottawa time) the last five seconds of countdown followed by an incredibly excited voice yelling over a terrific roar: "Four-three-two-one-ignition; LIFT OFF—LIFT OFF—LIFT OFF! The mighty Thor Agena B rocket heads straight up into the California night sky—STRAIGHT UP—STRAIGHT UP!" The roar then drowns me out for a moment or two.

The recording was played countless times on CFRA that day. Many listeners said it was one of the most exciting broadcasts they had ever heard. It was even replayed as part of a special commemorative display during at least one of the Alouette 1 anniversary celebrations, perhaps more.

Wait a minute, I can hear you say. You say Knowlton Nash of CBC was there to do a live broadcast as well. What happened to that?

Well, let me tell you.

As frequently happens, the launch was delayed for several days because of weather. While hanging around town, I picked up a fascinating story about a little fruit train that chugged through the Vandenberg Air Force Base whenever it felt like it. No schedule, no warning. All attempts by the base commander to have it rerouted had been thwarted by local politicians. If the train appeared during a countdown the launch very frequently had to be scrubbed, because of vibrations we were told. Plus there was a fear, believe it or not, that the train might be harbouring spies! Not so crazy when you think of it, since this was a major military base, dotted, you can be sure, with intercontinental ballistic missiles. An electrified fence and goodness knows what other security precautions surrounded the huge base, so this silly little train, carrying fruit from nearby farms to Los Angeles, posed a real security threat. Immediately after it appeared on the base, it would be followed by helicopters illuminating it with powerful floodlights until the caboose disappeared well down the tracks.

When I filed the story back to Ottawa, dubbing the fruit train the

Citrus Special, most news agencies simply didn't believe me and ignored the story—until about ten minutes before the first scheduled launch of Alouette 1, when what should appear on the base and cause it to be scrubbed? You guessed it, the Citrus Special!

This was too much for the CBC. Against the advice of Knowlton Nash, the giant brains at head office ordered Nash to pull up stakes at Vandenberg and cover another story somewhere in the American Midwest, thus leaving it all up to me with that jury-rigged microphone, the scorpions and snakes!

Even today, few Canadians understand what a truly magnificent accomplishment constructing that satellite was. With Alouette 1 bravely circling the earth, Canada took a giant leap forward in space technology. We, in fact, became the third country in the world after the USSR and USA to have built a successful satellite. Alouette was the cornerstone of Canada's giant leap to world leadership in the peaceful uses of space and upon which was built a competitive space industry that thrives to this day. Designed for only a one-year lifespan, Alouette 1 exceeded all expectations and was decommissioned, while still functioning, on its tenth anniversary. Until the 1970s, Alouette 1 was the satellite that provided information for more scientific publications than any other satellite in space. A plaque commemorating the engineering milestone is on display at the Shirley's Bay research site. It also commemorates the more than 100 people who worked on the Alouette program.

It is acknowledged today as one of the most successful scientific satellites ever and it ushered in a new era of scientific co-operation. Canadian scientists gained prominence as world experts, and in addition to Alouette 1 being designated as one of the ten most outstanding achievements in the first 100 years of engineering in Canada, in May of 1993, the global significance of the project was recognized when the Institute of Electrical and Electronic Engineers (IEEE), the largest technical organization in the world, designated Alouette 1 as an International Milestone of Electrical Engineering.

To be honest, I don't think my feat of engineering to get that broadcast on the air is all that shabby either! As a reward, CFRA decided to appoint my wife Kitty to be "Miss Alpine," as part of a major advertising campaign on behalf of a new cigarette brand. Fifty dollars a week for her to dress up like Heidi and hand out free samples from a big tray filled with Alpine cigarettes ("Cleaner, Cooler!"). Big money in those days—half as much as I was earning. With a three-month-old baby and a new house, heaven only knows we needed it!

The Valley Notebook

Behind me as I scoot up Highway 17 on that fateful escape trip to Ottawa from Montreal are a complicated lost love and a deadly boring job. What's ahead isn't nearly as clear. I have a job, that I know. CFRA's News Director, Campbell McDonald, says they can't wait to get me on board. But exactly what I will be doing and how much I'll be paid is far from settled. "I think Frank Ryan has something special in mind for you," says Campbell, as enthused as only he can be. "You'll have to work out the financial arrangement with him." "I won't come for less than $100 a week," I insist. "Oh well," says Campbell, "that shouldn't be a problem!"

But, of course, it was. "You want how much?!" asks an astonished Mr. Ryan, his eyes almost bugging out of his Coke-bottle glasses. "A hundred dollars a week!? We can't pay you that much. We don't pay Les Lye that much." I had no way of knowing how much Les Lye was making, and come to think of it I've never asked him. I did know that

Les was the big star at CFRA. I almost asked him how much they were paying Les' fantasy sidekick Abercrombie, but my first impression of Frank Ryan was that he wasn't the kind of guy you should be joking around with about money (an impression that never left me!).

If I had known what Frank had in mind for me, I would have held out for a lot more, but we finally reached an agreement. A hundred dollars a week, but that included Saturday mornings in the newsroom and I'd have to write the Valley Notebook for him. "What's the Valley Notebook?" I inquire.

"Ah," says Frank, "you can do it in your spare time. Probably half an hour at most. Just go through the Valley newspapers, clip out a few interesting items from each paper and make sure I get them before noon each Friday so I have time to record for the Sunday show."

First thing Monday morning I get the summons. A white-faced Campbell McDonald breaks the news. "Mr. Ryan wants to see you— right now!" I can see Campbell is worried. Is he going to lose his star newsman after only five days on the job?

As soon as I step into Frank's sprawling office, with its cowhide-covered desk, I know that in less than a week I've managed to do something that no sane person would really want to do in a lifetime: I've really, really ticked off Frank Ryan.

"What's this?" he says throwing a pile of newspaper clippings onto his desk? I don't have to look closely; I know very well what it is. "It's the Valley Notebook," I very foolishly reply. "THE VALLEY NOTEBOOK! THE VALLEY NOTEBOOK! THAT'S NOT THE VALLEY NOTEBOOK; THAT'S A PILE OF GARBAGE! NEXT TIME DO IT RIGHT!"

I am dismissed, somewhat relieved to know that at least there *is* to be a next time, but I'm totally befuddled. He asked for clippings from all the papers. I'd spent a couple of hours picking out some really interesting stuff, including a wedding announcement from the *Chesterville Record News* headlined "Hanke-Panke," which I thought was hilarious. Obviously, though, I was missing something important here.

It was Campbell McDonald, bless him, who explained it all. "Frank doesn't want anyone to know this, but his eyes aren't good enough anymore for him to read newsprint. You'll have to type up everything for him."

I was thunderstruck. "That will take hours. That will take me half a day to type up all that stuff—there's about 30 papers I have to go through." What I can't tell him, because what only Frank, our chief engineer and I are supposed know is that my other special assignment is to locate and secretly buy sufficient land in the Manotick area upon which to locate a whole new set of broadcast towers. Frank is smart enough to know that if anyone finds out what the land is for and who is really buying, the price will skyrocket.

It's Campbell again who finally comes to my rescue. He lines up a neighbour's daughter, a whiz-bang typist who, for five dollars a week, will do the typing for me.

When I explain it all to Kitty she is flabbergasted. "Let me get this straight," she says, "you're writing news five and a half days a week, sometimes half the night if there's a fire or a major accident. You spend half a day working on the Valley Notebook and you're scouring the country for a new transmitter site, all for a hundred dollars a week …and you've just taken a pay cut down to ninety-five?!"

I did the mathematics and had to admit she was right.

Horror From the Air

It was typical late November weather—cold and windy, with rain threatening to turn to snow. The kind of night you just want to bundle up in front of a fire with a good book. Our brand new house in Pte-Gatineau, just across the river from Ottawa, doesn't have a fireplace, but our pretty, blond-headed two-year-old Danielle has plunked herself on my knee insisting I read her *Green Eggs and Ham* for about the hundredth time. Lianne won't be along for about another five months; Kitty is having a much easier pregnancy this time. Life is good at the Greens'.

It's 6:30 p.m. on November 29, 1963. For 118 people aboard Trans-Canada Airlines (TCA) flight 138, leaving Montreal's Dorval Airport, life is about to end, suddenly.

All I know as I throw a few things into a suitcase is that a DC-8 aircraft has crashed near Ste-Thérèse de Blainville. As I am about to learn, the crash is only slightly more than a mile from where my father raised those famous Landrace Hogs and I helped Frank Selke, General Manager of the Montreal Canadiens, build his ramshackle chicken houses.

By the time I arrive at the outskirts of Ste-Thérèse, from listening to reports on Montreal radio stations, I know exactly where the plane has gone down. It was only a few years ago I hunted rabbits and woodcock in that bush and swamp. It gives me a great advantage over other reporters who are flocking to the scene, many of them uncertain about how to reach the site about half a mile in from the highway.

To compound their difficulty, reports of looting have prompted police to begin setting up roadblocks. I pull onto a rutted bush road I have walked many times in the past, and within minutes I'm in the midst of unspeakable horror. It is only too evident that the plane must have exploded before it hit the ground because well before I reach the main wreckage and the huge crater it has blasted into the swampy soil, the beam of my flashlight picks out things littering the ground and, as nightmares still remind me, in the trees, as well. Chunks of metal, blankets, clothes, a seat apparently undamaged dangling somehow from a branch. And other things so horrible I find it difficult even today to write about this tragic event.

Through the trees I can see streaks of light from other flashlights and at least one more powerful search light bouncing up into the upper branches and then criss-crossing in a desperate, and by now clearly hopeless, search for survivors. It is strangely funereal, the voices low, muffled by the snow and shock. One or two flashes of light flick toward me and dart quickly away as I reach the main crash site.

I learn later that the wreckage covered an area about half a mile long and about 250 feet wide. The crater measured 150 feet long by 75 feet wide. Trees in the immediate vicinity were smashed like matchsticks.

The DC-8 was the biggest of its kind in TCA (now Air Canada) service in 1963. It was en route to Toronto from Montreal's Dorval Airport, departing at 6:30 p.m. with 19-year veteran pilot Jack Snider in command. It crashed four minutes after takeoff.

By the time I arrive, heavy wet snow has begun to fall in huge flakes. Ambulances have been summoned from Ste-Thérèse and Montreal, but are soon cancelled when it becomes obvious there are no survivors. A request for police dogs to search for survivors is also cancelled.

I immediately begin to search for anyone who may have witnessed the plane as it plummeted to earth but am unsuccessful. Several nearby residents I speak with claim they were unaware of any problems until they heard a huge crash.

"I thought a big tanker truck must have smashed into a car or something," Marc Desjardins, a former neighbour of my father tells me.

Monty Adams, manager of the nearby Hillsdale Golf Club, says it sounded like an explosion or earthquake, but he couldn't tell exactly where it was until he spotted the glow from the flames. By the time I arrive, the flames have died out, but police on the scene tell me the wreckage and some of the nearby trees burned for more than two hours.

Realizing there was too much confusion at the site to learn anything more, and desperate to begin filing stories with CFRA, I check into a nearby motel in Ste-Thérèse, get busy on the phone to acquire more details, and subsequently file a four-minute story for the 11:00 p.m. news. I issue reports every hour after that until noon the next day. All, of course, by telephone.

When I return to the scene the next day, most of the wreckage and all of the bodies have been removed. Bulldozers have hacked a road from the main highway through the difficult terrain to provide official access to the site. No reporter can get within several hundred feet of the actual crash site, primarily because, according to police, people (including some reporters) had looted the site of various items. I saw nothing of the sort and have doubts that it actually happened. Former neighbours along Côte St-François that I spoke with later, claimed they couldn't imagine anyone doing such a thing.

The cause of this terrible crash, the worst ever on Canadian soil, has never been determined. According to a report of the Commission of Inquiry into the crash, conducted by the Department of Transportation and released in June of 1965, the most probable cause was mechanical failure of the pitch-trim compensator. This is the device that is used to regulate the nose up or down tendency of the aircraft.

Two years ago, I revisited the crash site to find a small memorial garden near the Ste-Thérèse parish cemetery. It's quite beautiful and peaceful with several stone benches and two huge boulders that they claim were dug from the site where the crash occurred. Nearby is a granite monument with the names of the 111 passengers and 11 crew members who died that horrible night. I was very moved by it. I had planned on finding that old road through the bush and revisiting the crash site, but something held me back. Too many ghosts, perhaps.

People often ask me if covering tragedies of this sort haunt me. I have to confess that, as with other journalists who have had similar experiences, you do develop a kind of callous shell. Not unlike that acquired, I suspect, by doctors who have to deal with death and dying on a regular basis. For some reason, however, I still occasionally have nightmares about the Ste-Thérèse crash. Perhaps it is because it occurred so close to where I used to live, but more likely, some psychiatrists have told me, it is because I fly frequently and thus can imagine myself coming to such a sudden and horrific death.

On the other hand, my coverage of the Springhill Mine disaster in the fall of 1958 had much more of an emotional drain on me at the time, but because I could never imagine myself in a coal mine, the effects have not been as lasting.

Generally during live broadcasts, adrenaline takes over and I am able to keep my emotions at bay. I must confess, though, that some of the stories I wrote for United Press International during the Springhill Mine disaster (covered in detail in my first memoir, *The Pork Chop and Other Stories*) were pounded out on an old typewriter more than a little dampened by tears. There were very few dry eyes to be found, amongst relatives, townsfolk or reporters during the dramatic rescues at Springhill.

I saw no tears, however, at the Ste-Thérèse crash site. Toronto's airport was the place where news of this tragic event had been released, and the victims' families and loved ones, for the most, had gathered there or at Dorval.

While it remains the worst airplane crash ever on Canadian soil, the story has been largely forgotten, overshadowed even at the time, by the aftermath of another tragic event that November: the assassination of President John F. Kennedy on November 22, exactly one week prior to the crash.

The President Is Dead!

There is an ancient saying that the bells ring only three times for a man: when he is born, when he marries and when he dies. When he dies, it is the death knell that announces the grim news. I often think of that because it was the sound of urgently ringing bells that first alerted us at CFRA, and thus much of the City of Ottawa, to one of the most tragic events in history.

Try as I might, I can recall nothing of November 22, 1963, until 12:32 p.m. I don't remember what the weather was like, I don't know why I was still in the newsroom at CFRA, I don't know where our other newsmen were. It is as though something has wiped the blackboard of my mind clear until the bells on our UPI Teletype machine begin an urgent ringing at exactly two minutes past the bottom of the noon hour.

Today, of course, radio and television newsrooms are entirely computerized. Teletype machines have long ago been supplanted by satellite feeds from around the world. I may be the last broadcaster on the face of the planet who still reads from hard copy and not a computer screen. I gave up my typewriter only a couple of years ago.

But in the fall of 1963, high tech in a radio newsroom means that when there is urgent breaking news someplace in the world your Teletype machine gives a two- or three-second ring of its bell. If the news is deemed to be a bulletin, more vital than just urgent, it gives two or three rings of perhaps four or five seconds each. But when the bell rings continuously for several minutes, your blood runs cold. This, don't forget, is the height of the Cold War! We have only just begun to sleep properly again after the Cuban Missile Crisis!

But it isn't an incoming warhead the frantically ringing Teletype bell announces on this grim November afternoon. From that moment on, I can recall everything with perfect clarity, almost as though it was yesterday.

My heart pounding, I jump from my desk and throw open the wooden sliding door leading to the cramped Teletype room and rip off those dreadful words: (UPI) Nov. 22—12.32—FLASH—FLASH—PRESIDENT KENNEDY SHOT—DALLAS—MORE.

These shocking words in hand, I race down the hallway to the studio where News Director Campbell McDonald has just begun the 12:30 news. Throwing open the double doors leading to the studio, I grasp the sitting Campbell by his right shoulder, almost yank him off his chair, away from the microphone and hand him the story. Not waiting to see his reaction, I immediately turn and dash back to the newsroom for further details.

Campbell is an old pro, as experienced and poised a broadcaster as exists in Canada at the time, and despite his obvious shock at my sudden intrusion and the dreadful news, he immediately discards the rest of his newscast and in a calm voice tells his listeners that the President of the United States has been shot in Dallas, Texas. "We do not know how seriously," he says, "please stay tuned for all the details as they become available." He then begins to ad lib what information he can recall concerning President Kennedy's trip to Texas.

Back in the newsroom, I rifle through piles of back copy, dig out background information concerning the trip, rip off more current information from both the UPI and Canadian Press news wires which now inform us that Kennedy has been shot in the head during his motorcade ride through Dallas and has been rushed to hospital. The wires say that Texas Governor John Connally has also been shot.

I continue to race up and down that hallway from the newsroom to the studio, supplying Campbell with every shred of information I can gather. It is shortly after 1:00 p.m. when the UPI bells begin their frantic ringing again. The news is terrible, but not really a surprise. (UPI) Nov. 22—1.14PM—FLASH—PRESIDENT KENNEDY CONFIRMED DEAD.

Walter Cronkite can't hold back tears when announcing the news to the American people on television. Try as we might, neither can Campbell McDonald nor I as we break the terrible news to our listeners in Ottawa and the Valley.

Regular programming on CFRA is cancelled for the rest of the day as Campbell and I continue broadcasting the shocking events.

Minutes before the official confirmation of Kennedy's death, Dallas patrolman J. D. Tippit is shot and killed while questioning a man on the street. The man is seen by at least a dozen people, running into a nearby theatre. Police converge on the scene and arrest Lee Harvey Oswald, a Marine Corps vet who had once been hired as an order taker at the Texas School Book Depository from where it is surmised the fatal shots have been fired.

At 2:15 p.m., the President's body is in a casket and loaded onto Air Force One for the return flight to Washington. The takeoff is delayed while Federal Judge Sarah Hughes swears in Lyndon B. Johnson as the 36th President of a shocked United States.

Who can forget those pictures of Jackie Kennedy, still in clothing stained by her husband's blood, standing beside Johnson during the swearing-in ceremony?

Many years later, during a tour of Washington, I found myself very moved when the tour guide pointed out the church steps upon which John F. Kennedy Jr. (John John) stood and saluted his daddy's casket as it passed by. John Kennedy Jr., of course, died a tragic death himself, as did the President's brother Bobby Kennedy.

Some say the Kennedy assassination signaled the end of innocence. I don't know about that, but to paraphrase a popular song of the day the times they were a changing! Soon to follow were the Civil Rights Movement, the assassinations of Dr. Martin Luther King and Bobby Kennedy, the Women's Liberation Movement, Vietnam…and let's not forget the Pill and the Beatles!

It was neither the best of times nor the worst of times, but it most certainly was the most interesting of times, and it was into that tumultuous decade that I was soon to launch one of the most interesting and tumultuous radio programs in Canada's history!

Son of Jumbo

In our brave new world, where a sizable portion of our population is desperate to find something to be offended by, I am a little hesitant to tell you this story, but what the heck. At this stage in my life and career, what can they do to me? It was all in fun, no one got hurt, and besides, a lot of people got a big kick out of it. Some people even made a pile of money.

It's been so long ago I don't recall whether it was my idea or that of Morrison Arnott. Moe, as we all affectionately called him, was CFRA's City Hall reporter, famous for his ability to mimic the high-pitched voice of Mayor Charlotte Whitton. Roly-poly, affable, curious with twinkling, intelligent eyes buried behind horn-rimmed glasses, Moe became my first friend in Ottawa. In fact, he was my best man about a year later when I married Kitty.

Even though station owner Frank Ryan insisted we always use the phrase "CFRA on the Queensway," when I arrived in the fall of 1960, it was railway tracks that lay just across the street from our yellow brick building at 150 Isabella Street. The Queensway wasn't completed along that centretown stretch until about a year later.

One fine September day, not long after my arrival in Ottawa, Moe and I watch with great interest from our third-floor newsroom window as several specially built boxcars are shunted onto the tracks almost directly beneath us. The circus is coming to nearby Lansdowne Park and a whole zoo-load of exotic animals is being unloaded and parked on our doorstep. As an exceptionally large elephant clomps onto the pavement and lets rip with a trumpet blast, we look at each other, grab a tape recorder and head out in hopes of a story

The guy in charge looks like he's spent a night or two in the lion's cage. Wild eyes, an ugly looking welt on his neck, long scraggly hair, obviously just fresh from mud wrestling, and with an accent so thick no sane person could possibly understand him. We do our best. I poke my microphone as close to him as I dare. "How big is that elephant? What's his name?"

There follows about three minutes of what sounds to me like gibberish. A combination of highland Scottish and lowland South African dialects perhaps? With just a hint maybe of Jamaican? Sometimes if you listen closely and long enough to a very broad accent you can begin to decipher certain words, so I try again. "Where does he come from and what did you says his name was?" "Ahdinkecomfralawnolrexsizizrnim," or something like that, is the reply. I'm startled as Moe pipes up, "He comes from the London Zoo, you say?" "Azarazlo."

This goes on for several minutes. I don't understand a word. Moe seems to find the guy crystal clear, but when we listen to the tape recording back in the newsroom, it's apparent even to Moe that listeners won't be able to make head nor tail of any of it. "Too bad," says Moe, "old Rex is a pretty interesting character, could even be related to Jumbo."

I'm confused. "Did he say the elephant's name is Rex? I sure didn't pick that out, but what's the story about Jumbo? Are you talking about the Jumbo that was killed by a train in St. Thomas? Holy cats, I learned about that in grade one. That was back before the turn of the century!"

"Actually," says Moe, "Jumbo was killed in 1885. But he was in the London Zoo before that and our friend out there claims Rex was born there about a year after old P. T. Barnum bought Jumbo and shipped him off to his circus on this side of the big pond." I can see a gleam in Moe's eye. "Why don't we do a story raising the possibility that Rex is Jumbo's son? It wouldn't be entirely dishonest. It would make a heck of a story. By the way, did you know that Jumbo is actually an African word for elephant?"

What we finally decide is more ambitious and yes, I admit, far more deceitful.

Moe, after a bit of practice, creates a wonderfully thick but very understandable accent—a kind of cross between Charlotte Whitton and John Diefenbaker. I introduce him on tape as world-famous elephant trainer Doctor Morley Aronson, and conduct an interview that to the best of memory goes something like the following:

Lowell: Doctor Aronson, welcome to Ottawa.

Moe: Thank you; it is a great pleasure to visit your beautiful city.

Lowell: Doctor, you are here with one of the largest elephants I have ever seen. Tell us a little about Rex.

Moe: Yes. I have known Rex—have trained that magnificent animal—now for almost 15 years. It is a great honour because, as you know, Rex is the only living progeny of that most famous of all huge elephants, Jumbo.

Lowell: But Jumbo was killed by a train in St. Thomas, Ontario, in 1885. When and where did he sire Rex?"

Moe: As you know, Mr. Green, Jumbo was born in Ethiopia in 1861 and arrived at the London Zoo a few years later. He lived there, giving great joy to children, for 17 years. It was during that time that he was mated with a wonderful female elephant named Rita who gave birth to Rex shortly after Jumbo was bought by Mr. P. T. Barnum and shipped to North America as the star of his world-famous circus, the Greatest Show on Earth.

Lowell: But, Doctor Aronson, that would make Rex here more than 70 years of age. Elephants usually don't live much beyond 70.

Moe: We have taken excellent care of Rex. He will be 77 years of age tomorrow, as a matter of fact. We are holding a special birthday party for him here in Ottawa.

Lowell: When he died, Jumbo was a bit over 11 feet tall. How tall is his son Rex?"

Moe: Rex is exactly ten feet, seven and three quarter inches tall, believed to be the tallest elephant alive in the world today.

Lowell: Amazing. Thank you very much. We have been speaking with Doctor Morley Aronson, world-famous elephant trainer about the world-famous son of Jumbo—the great and noble pachyderm Rex, now here in Ottawa to celebrate his 77th birthday. We wish Rex happy birthday and plenty of peanuts."

The hardest part of the interview was not killing ourselves laughing. At first we hesitated to actually play it on air, but decided, what the heck. I mean it could be true, right?

The story caused great excitement. I don't think anyone ever caught on, although News Director Campbell McDonald gave both of us a strange, raised-eyebrows look. The circus never complained. Why would they? Attendance set records, and the birthday elephant was showered the next day with peanuts. Somebody even brought a peanut-butter cake, which apparently Rex devoured with one inhale.

Thousands of people still visit the life-sized statue of Jumbo in St. Thomas each year. It is one of the main tourist attractions in that town, just south of London. As for Rex, we never heard of him again. Moe tried to track him down once, but when he phoned Ringling Brothers Barnum and Bailey Circus headquarters in Florida they didn't seem to know what he was talking about.

Moe and I promised each other we'd never tell the world what we did way back in 1960, but while writing this book I was suddenly struck with an idea. Was that elephant's name really Rex? Did Moe make up the whole thing? I couldn't understand a word that shaggy-haired elephant trainer had to say. Was Moe only pretending he understood? To be honest with you, I wouldn't put it past Moe one little bit. He once tried to spread the word that I really hadn't broad-cast the launch of Alouette 1 from California but had, in fact, faked it from an empty barrel in the CFRA garage. Was the biggest joke of all played on me? Sadly, Moe isn't with us anymore to set the record straight. The good really do die far too young.

Retaliation

Dean Hagopian was the big name in Ottawa radio in the early 1960s. One-time lead singer with the Staccatos, a semi-famous local band, he began drawing huge teen audiences to his "Solid Gold" show on CKOY. In truth, he was kicking our butt at CFRA in the ratings war. Even worse, he gloated about it on air. A night seldom passed without Dean making some derogatory remark about "the farmers" or "old fogies" listening to CFRA.

I didn't mind too much as long as he didn't sharpen his tongue on my hide. But when I started filling in on "Farmer's Notebook" for Frank Ryan, Dean launched a little skit in which he would pretend to welcome me to his show as a special guest, and then begin to make barnyard sounds. I have to confess his impression of a cow in desperate need of milking (or something) was reasonably accurate.

When a few friends picked up on this and began mooing in my presence, I decided enough was enough. I picked up the phone and dialed Dean Hagopian at his CKOY office.

Affecting the best Bert Cannings voice and bluster I could muster, I said "Dean, Bert Cannings here, CFCF Montreal. Was driving through town yesterday. Picked up your show. Loved it. Our General Manager here wants to talk to you. Be in my office at eight tomorrow morning. I'll introduce you. By the way, salaries here for our stars start at ten thousand! Tomorrow morning—eight sharp—don't be late!" And hung up.

You know what happened.

Bert Cannings, never the most pleasant of personalities, was especially bearish in the early morning. He threw Dean out of his office with a warning never to set foot in Montreal again!

I thought this was hilarious and boasted about it all over CFRA. Big mistake! Someone squealed.

At about three o'clock the next morning came a pounding on my door. Someone had ordered four large pizzas to be delivered to my address.

The next morning at about the same time, it was an ambulance, siren blaring, attendants demanding to know where the heart attack victim was.

The worst was a deliveryman from a local grocery store who dropped about a hundred dollars' worth of groceries on my front porch and demanded payment.

The next day I phoned Dean back. "Okay," I said, "I give up!"

He claimed he had no idea what I was talking about, but the nightly visits stopped. Dean went on to greater things, making a major name for himself with Montreal radio (not CFCF!) and then later as an actor and movie producer. A major talent and worthy foe!

Hijinks

Today broadcasting is all serious, all money, all the time. But in the 1950s and '60s, the favourite game in radio and, to a lesser degree, in television was "break up the announcer." Virtually anything you could do to break the announcer's concentration and get him (announcers were pretty well all male then) to burst into laughter on air was fair game.

The best I ever saw at this game was Bill Brady, morning man at CKPC Brantford before he went on to much greater fame in London. When I started in Brantford radio in the fall of 1956, Bill was at the top of his game. We didn't have an announcer on staff who hadn't been reduced, on air, to a bowl of quivering, laughing jelly at one of Bill's hijinks. Except for one.

Arnold Anderson was a Brantford institution for decades, one of the best local sports announcers I have ever heard. A man who claimed his powers of concentration were so great that he was incapable of being broken up on air. "You just can't do it," he boasted to Bill Brady one day. "There's nothing in the world you can do that will break me up once I punch that microphone on!"

It was a boast he should never have made, because for the next several months, Bill Brady just about drove him crazy. One of Bill's favourite tricks was to bring a small child's chair into the studio, and plunk himself down on it directly in front of Arnold's desk as he read his noon sportscast. If Arnold were to glance up, all he would see above the desk was the top of Bill Brady's head and two eyes peering at him through horn-rimmed glasses only a few inches away. That didn't work. Not even a grin from Arnold.

From somewhere, Bill acquired a brightly coloured grass skirt and Hawaiian lei. But not even a bare belly and hairy-legged hula dance would do it. Arnold Anderson delivered his sportscast flawlessly.

There were various other attempts, some quite breathtaking in their inventiveness, but Arnold was unflappable—disdainful even of Bill's strikeouts.

"Amateur," claimed Arnold one fateful day, "the man's an obvious amateur."

"So he thinks I'm an amateur, does he?" mused Bill, when informed of the slander. "Boys, be sure to tune in tomorrow!"

And so we all did, peering through the window from the control room as Bill Brady waits for Arnold Anderson to sign on with his noon sports. Arnold signs on as Bill strolls into the studio with a brown paper bag, from which he slowly extracts a small blow torch. Watching closely, we can see Arnold's eyes widen a bit at this. From his pocket, Bill pulls a lighter, flicks it on, slowly turns a knob on the blowtorch, and then presto a geyser of blue flame erupts. Arnold still hasn't missed a beat, but a careful listener could easily discern that his breathing is more rapid than usual. It is no contest, however, when Bill leans over and very carefully lights fire to the bottom of the script from which Arnold is reading. In the end, Arnold claims it was he who actually won since he was too busy beating out the flames to laugh.

The challenge probably would have resumed if CKPC's owner Mrs. Buchanan, smelling smoke and fearing the worst in the old house that housed our studios, hadn't come running in and put a stop to it all. "Act like grown-ups," she scolds.

I'll never forget Bill Brady's response. "But Mrs. B, we can't act like grown-ups, we're in radio!"

I Almost Kill Jim Marino

I loved Jim Marino, but he drove me crazy. Happy-go-lucky, with an infectious smile and a million jokes, he was the life of any party, but as our afternoon news announcer at CFRA in the mid to late '60s, he pestered me so much I banned him from the newsroom. Not that it made any difference. You could be certain that a good half hour before the newscast, Jim would come shuffling, full speed, down the hall and barge, unannounced and uninvited, into the tiny newsroom, shouting, "Where's my newscast?" The reply was always the same. "Get lost Marino! It'll be ready in 20 minutes, so buzz off and leave me alone!"

Jim would do a little spinarama, chuckle and shuffle off. And when I say shuffle, I mean shuffle. Full speed, oh yes, but never bother lifting your feet! You could hear him half a mile away. And you'd hear him again in about two minutes. A burst into the newsroom again: "Where's my newscast?" The same response, more heated this time. This little performance was staged three or four times an hour.

To make matters worse, in those days the newsroom at CFRA

wasn't much larger than the Alcatraz jail cell that accommodated the Birdman and Machine Gun Kelly! Who ever designed the building must have been a madman, since some huge object was suspended in the ceiling, with an uncanny resemblance to the keel of a boat. Moe Arnott claimed he had proof it was in fact the keel of the *Titanic*!

Jam two Teletype machines, several typewriters, a couple of desks and some filing cabinets in, and there was barely room for me in there, let alone a shuffling Jim Marino driving me crazy with demands for his newscast every five minutes.

Banning him from the newsroom was totally ineffective. Jim didn't care much for rules. So I got the bright idea to lock him out.

I managed to convince someone in our workshop to convert the newsroom door into a Dutch door. The bottom half would be locked, keeping Marino out. He could swing the top half open to make his usual inquiries and to get his newscast when it was ready, but his barging-into-the-newsroom days would be over.

The workshop managed to get the job done during a weekend. They even put an especially strong bolt on the bottom half, which I was informed would stop a raging buffalo.

Well, it certainly stopped a shuffling Jim Marino. At least the bottom half of Jim Marino. Totally unaware of the new configuration, Jim came speed shuffling down the corridor, and before my brain registered the danger, he threw open the door and barged in.

Except this time, of course, his bottom half didn't barge. In fact, it didn't budge. His top half, on the other hand, made it in, as far as his bottom half would allow. There was a huge ufffff, a cry of pain and several words I do not wish to repeat, including several which I believe were Italian.

There was no serious damage, although for the next several days the shuffle was replaced by a very definite hobble.

Aside from his Dutch door "dive," Jim Marino will be best remembered by many of you as the voice behind "I.G.A.—I Give Away." Hundreds of entries poured into CFRA from I.G.A. shoppers every day. All were placed in a large drum, into which Jim Marino would reach several times a day to pick the winner of various grocery products.

The problem with this was that Jim was hardly the most coordinated guy in the world. One afternoon, while reaching especially deep into the drum, he fell off his stool and partially into the drum. Please keep in mind this was all live radio. I didn't actually hear that episode, but from all reports it was a radio classic.

I remember meeting Jim in the hallway one day where he excitedly told me he had just met the woman he was going to marry. "Geez," I said, "that's great, Jim. What's her name? Do I know her?"

He gave me one of his little chuckles. "Well, to tell the truth, I only just saw her on the bus this morning. I don't know her name yet, but I'll tell you tomorrow."

I forget if he did discover her name that quickly, but this I do know: he married her.

Jim Marino went on to take up another occupation and became Mayor of St. Catharines. I've lost touch with him, but understand he's still shuffling along just fine!

Death on a Bridge

Mayor Ron Reid is a big man. Well over six feet, with broad shoulders and a thick chest. On most days he looks as if he could suit up as a linesman with the Ottawa Rough Riders, but tonight he looks shrunken, his face is pale and drawn, and his hand trembles slightly as he shakes mine. "This is terrible, Lowell," he says, "awful. We've got at least five, maybe six, killed, dozens injured. Some men even jumped into the river, for God's sake!" Could they survive that? He shakes his head. "No one seems to know." Someone calls for him and the Mayor is gone.

The morning of Wednesday, August 10, 1966, started out a bit foggy, especially along the Rideau River, as dozens of construction workers began pouring concrete onto the south span of the soon-to-be-completed $2.4 million Heron Road Bridge spanning the Rideau River and the Rideau Canal about a mile south of the Hog's Back Bridge. By noon the fog had burned off, and some of the workmen removed shirts as the temperature reached the mid-80s Fahrenheit.

Those who were there at the time tell me the talk and bantering on the worksite was a little more animated than usual. It was a beautiful day, and a few of the men planned to attend a friend's backyard birthday barbecue later in the evening. The job was nearing completion, and because the work of pouring concrete at the eastern end of the southern span was progressing so well, it looked as though they'd be able to finish up by the 4:30 quitting time.

One of the men told me he had just checked his pocket watch to see that it was exactly 3:30 when, without warning, there was a sudden violent shudder, and then a loud roar as the entire west slab of hardened concrete, laid almost a month previously, flipped over in a giant, deadly somersault directly onto the east slab where the men were working.

Some of the men were killed instantly or severely injured by falling slabs of rock-hard concrete from the western section that fell directly on top of them. Others were driven down into the mass of wet concrete they had just laid and were buried alive.

Eyewitnesses say it was a scene of absolute horror. Screams for help, moans of pain, and a huge cloud of dust that obscured everything.

My open-line show, "The Greenline," would not be born for another month. I had wrapped up a news and editorial shift at 1:00 p.m., picked up five-year-old Danielle and three-year-old Lianne from the babysitter's house and was just pulling into the laneway of our home near Wakefield, Quebec, when I heard the first bulletin on CFRA. I immediately returned my daughters to the babysitter, phoned Kitty at our pet shop on Sparks Street with the news, and then rushed to the scene.

The first person I met was Reverend George Larose, chaplain of the Ottawa Fire Department, who had been saying the last rites over some of those killed. There were tears in his eyes. "At least seven dead that we know of," he told me. "Some of the injured won't likely make it." It was he who told me that workers had used their hard hats to scoop wet concrete away from some of the trapped men. I later learned that one of those thus saved was George Veiga, who was submerged almost up to his neck in wet concrete with the arms of a dead co-worker wrapped around his legs.

By the time I arrive and begin broadcasting, most of the injured— more than 50 in all—have been rushed to hospital, some in ambulances, others in taxis which appeared on the scene to assist, and some in private cars. A military helicopter has also been used to ferry the injured to nearby hospitals.

Rescue operations continue well into the night as giant floodlights illuminate a ghostly scene of chaos and despair. Shattered wooden timbers, large chunks of hardened concrete dangling from broken and twisted steel reinforcing rods. A few yellow hard hats scattered about, a boot, flashing red lights from nearby police and rescue vehicles. Until well past midnight, cutting torches and metal-cutting saws send up showers of sparks as workers search frantically for more survivors.

Finally, at about 2:00 a.m., rescue operations are called off. No more men are found alive.

Seven were killed at the site. Another worker died shortly after in hospital, a ninth died about a month later. Many of the 55 who were injured never fully recovered. It is the worst construction accident in Ottawa's history.

The bridge was rebuilt and opened to traffic on April 16, 1968. The names of those killed in the disaster are engraved on a plaque that, in turn, is embedded in a large boulder that can be found today just west of the bridge on Heron Road.

I have always believed that if "The Greenline" had been on the air at that time, the workers would not have been treated as shabbily as most were. There is no question that far more pressure should have been applied to the contractor, the city and the province to properly compensate the family members of those who were killed or seriously injured. Believe it or not, the general contractor, O. J. Gaffney Ltd. of Stratford, was fined only $5,000, despite the findings of an inquiry that the cause of the collapse was the use of green timber and the lack of diagonal bracing on the wooden support forms.

In addition to the token fine, two engineers were suspended from their jobs, and a third was reprimanded. And that's it, nothing more. Unbelievable!

The families of workers killed on the job got compensation of a miserly few hundred dollars a month. Many of the injured workers, including some severely injured, never received a cent.

Had "The Greenline" been on the air, we may not have been able to get a better deal for the workers and their families, but by God, of this you can be certain: If we had gone down to any defeat it would have been with all guns blazing! The entire city would have been in an uproar over the terrible treatment dished out to the workers. As it was, barely a popgun was fired in defence of justice for those, who through the negligence and incompetence of others, lost their health, their lives or their loved ones. It was not one of the prouder moments in the history of Ottawa—or of Ontario.

Born to Talk Radio

When a child is born, it is a joyful event, carefully noted with oohs and aahs, balloons, flowers, official records and baby pictures affixed to fridge magnets. The launching of even the most insignificant of ships warrants a bottle of champagne across the bow. With all that in mind, I suggested that, at the very least, CFRA should spring for a case of beer to celebrate the birth of "The Greenline," but no such luck. A round of ham and tomato sandwiches in our cafeteria was the best we could come up with. I suppose I can't blame management, because for all anyone knew, this new talk show with Lowell Green hosting might not last the week. Heck, it might not even last the first day!

Let's face it, an open-line show, even in 1966, was really pushing the envelope. A mighty risky experiment at a time when Ed Sullivan still wouldn't let us have a look at Elvis below the hips! League of Decency campaigns were being launched against stations daring to play the Beatles, for heaven's sake!

Fortunately, when I punched on the microphone for that first "Greenline" program, I really didn't understand how precarious my situation was. In all likelihood, all it would have taken would have been for one major sponsor, or perhaps even one of station owner Kathleen Ryan's friends, to object to something I said to have the whole thing canned.

There was virtually no promotion for the launch of the show, which in the first several years only ran from 1:05 p.m. until 2:00 p.m.

As a matter of fact, I have been unable to find a single newspaper ad promoting that first show, and as another illustration of how insignificant we considered it, I cannot even tell you the exact date "The Greenline" started. I know it was the summer of 1966, but beyond that, despite the fact that the show went on to become one of the most successful and longest running radio talk shows in North America, for the life of me, I can't tell you its birthdate.

The reason I can remember the guest featured on that first show is because he was the man who introduced me to my first wife.

Don Shaw had a beautiful mellifluous voice, and when well, he was an excellent announcer reading news and commercials. He became a good friend, and despite the fact I was still smarting from my hasty exodus from Montreal and had sworn off beautiful women, Don persuaded me to join Ottawa's famous Orpheus Operatic Society where, he claimed, "good looking women are hanging from the rafters!" Never having seen that kind of thing before, I ambled on down to their little building near the Grace Hospital one night to have a peek at those rafters. Before I knew it, I was onstage

We didn't know if "The Greenline" would last its first day on the air, so the historic launch went virtually unnoticed. It was only after a few months, as ratings began to soar, that station management decided there might be a future for talk radio, after all! This *Citizen* ad gave people in Ottawa a first look at the guy they were growing to love—or hate!

as Rufe, a dumb hillbilly in the Orpheus April 1961 production of *Li'l Abner*. Little did I know what Daisy Mae had in store for me!

We had been in rehearsals for a couple of weeks, when the phone rang one memorable night in my little bachelor's walk-up apartment on Delaware Avenue. "I keep dreaming about you every night," the voice said. It was the star of the show, Daisy Mae, with dumb hillbilly Rufe dumbstruck on the other end of the line. Less than a year later Claudette (Kitty) Boivin and Lowell Green were married and remained that way for more than 19 years, raising two wonderful daughters.

• • •

When CFRA General Manager Terry Kielty agreed to launch "The Greenline" in order to prevent me from accepting an offer from Hal Anthony of CKOY to host their open-line show "Live Wire," I was determined to do something other than just the usual "fluff" or "shock" formats that were in vogue at the time. So I called my old friend Don Shaw, who had drifted in and out of our lives for the past several years.

I explained to him what was happening and asked if he would be willing to make some history and be the first guest on the first edition of "The Greenline" and to tell his story. Without hesitation, he agreed.

And so it was that Don Shaw and I broke some new ground during that first show, as he candidly, and with a total absence of self-pity, told of his monumental struggles with bipolar disease, including the electroshock therapy he frequently had to undergo. It was a far cry from the usual fare served up by talk shows of the day, and the reviews were laudatory. It may be one of the few programs I ever conducted during which at least one complaint wasn't lodged. Although in those days people didn't seem as anxious to be offended.

When it was all over, I realized that I had not been the least bit nervous. Terry Kielty, in a rare congratulatory move, came into the studio to shake hands with both of us, very graciously thanking us. He then turned to me and said something much more prophetic than I suspected at the time. "Lowell," he said, "you were born to do talk radio!"

Over the more than 40 years since that day, I have lost track of Don Shaw. Sadly, I fear, fate has not treated him nearly as well as it has me.

A Very Public Flogging

In my earlier memoir, *The Pork Chop and Other Stories*, I wrote that "life is far too great an adventure, far too much fun to spend much effort or ink rooting around in the bad times," but on second thought it is probably time to do a bit of rooting into one of the most painful events in my broadcasting career. It's a story that has never before been told but should be, since it's a fairly important chapter in the history of Ottawa. Out of respect for some of those involved, I will avoid using the names of most of those involved. The details are as I recall them, although most of the facts are there for anyone who cares to delve further into this rather sordid, shameful tale of labour union machinations.

If I had known what lay ahead when Reverend Norm Johnson walked into my life inquiring whether I was "just all talk," I would surely have turned him down flat.

It's the summer of 1970; "The Greenline" is flourishing. You'd be hard pressed to find any adult in Ottawa who doesn't tune in at least occasionally, either to nod in agreement or drop kick the radio through the living room!

"There's a Reverend Norman Johnson who insists on seeing you," says our receptionist. "What do you want me to say?" "Does he look like he's crazy or armed?" I ask, only half jokingly. There's a pause as she checks the Reverend out a little more closely. "Looks okay to me," she whispers into the phone. "Okay, send him up," I whisper back and hang up.

The Reverend, which is what we all came to call him, certainly doesn't look threatening. Medium height, medium build, short sandy-coloured hair, a decent enough moustache and a right hand, which when he sticks it out to shake yours, you discover is missing a couple of fingers. Within a few minutes, you learn that he's an alcoholic who's been dry for several years and a man who's almost impossible to say no to.

"That program you were running today," he says, "did you mean it when you said we've got to do something about fatherless boys running wild?" What could I say? "Of course, I meant it," I reply, "and it's not just fatherless kids either. If we don't do something about drugs in our schools and playgrounds, we're headed for big trouble."

The Reverend looks me straight in the eye. "Good. I'm glad you just aren't all talk because I want you to help me form a branch of Big Brothers here in Ottawa. Are you up for it?"

And that's how it started. The next day I went on the air appealing to anyone interested in coming on board as a director to call me. The response was terrific, and within a few weeks we had recruited more than a dozen men, including business leaders, lawyers, public servants, even a leading artist.

From Big Brothers organizations in other communities we obtained information concerning methods of operation, but we had no money, no staff, no office, and not even a place to meet. These we had to find on our own. One of our group members managed to persuade the

NCC to loan us an unused office for our first meeting. We arrived that night with great hopes, only to find that the office was locked and no one had a key. Someone managed to scramble up over the top of a disgustingly dusty wall to open the door, and Big Brothers of Ottawa was officially launched with me as President.

Our first job was to raise sufficient money to rent an office, hire some staff and start matching fatherless boys with volunteer men ready to provide some much needed male role modelling and mentoring. As you can appreciate, finding appropriate matches is a very delicate matter; pitfalls, as we were to learn, abound.

An earlier attempt at operating a Big Brothers association in Ottawa failed shortly after the Second World War amid charges of sexual abuse of some of the boys. Memories tend to be very keen in Ottawa, so any stumble out of the gate this time would probably kill the idea of Big Brothers in our city for decades. The screening process had to be very thorough.

All of us worked tirelessly to raise enough money to hire a top-notch professional. We tried bottle drives, went door-to-door, twisted friends' arms and met with dozens of representatives from various service clubs and church groups. The Civitan Club helped with a snowmobile endurance run, which my kidneys still complain about! The United Way was approached, but we were informed that we would have to raise the money on our own for several years before they could become involved.

Someone came up with the idea of bingos, so we strapped on aprons and fought our way through a thick haze of smoke night after night. We held a giant bingo at the Civic Centre one night with almost a thousand people in attendance, every one of whom I swear, seemed to be smoking three cigarettes at a time! That's when they weren't giving us hell. I remember one fine gentleman giving me a tongue-lashing because the numbers on one of his cards were identical to those held by someone else at his table. I was so stupid I didn't know this was fairly common and the reason there is sometimes more than one winner per game.

I don't really know why, but we never seemed to get much money from any of the bingos. By the time all the winnings were paid out, along with hall rental, and so on, we often ended up with a pittance.

Then one of the city's top artists, Charlie Spratt, suggested an art auction with himself donating some of his finest work. The auctions, with Ken "The General" Grant as auctioneer, and if memory serves me right, Dave Smith upon occasion, were a great success, and finally we were on the way. Or so we thought.

We rented a small office above a restaurant on Elgin Street, appointed what we believed was an experienced Executive Director, and then, with his approval, hired a graduate social worker and began making matches. By this time dozens of mothers had approached us desperate to find a Big Brother to match up with their sons. The Board's instructions to our staff were to match as quickly as possible, but each match had to be very carefully screened and monitored. We could make no mistakes, especially in the early days when the entire community would be watching us very closely.

As our fundraising efforts continued to improve, our Executive Director hired a young male student from Carleton University's School of Social Work to assist in office work.

Then it hit the fan!

At some point during this period, several representatives from a gay men's association in Ottawa approached our Executive Director requesting a meeting with all the "little brothers." This request was brought forward to the Board of Directors. We instructed our Executive Director that under no circumstances was there to be any meeting between a gay male association and any "little brother." Most of our members could see no reason for Big Brothers of Ottawa to be involved in arranging any meeting of any kind between "little brothers" and *any* organization. The matches were private matters involving only our organization, the "big brother" involved, and the boy and his mother.

Despite our specific instructions, our Executive Director defied us and arranged at least one, and perhaps more, meetings between representatives of a local gay men's organization and one or more "little brothers." To this day, I have no idea why.

When the Board was informed of this, we were naturally very disturbed and demanded an explanation. Our Executive Director said he could see no harm in the meetings and had decided on his own to allow them. "I am the professional," he reminded us. At that meeting he was once again instructed not to arrange any more such meetings under any circumstances. He was informed at that time of what had caused the demise of the first attempt at forming a Big Brothers organization in Ottawa.

We believed then that the matter had ended. That is, until a few days later when one of our Board members informed us that he had made an unannounced visit to our Elgin Street office the day before, only to see our Executive Director and the young male employee "wrestling" on the floor!

We immediately served notice to our Executive Director that his services were terminated. Now it was *really* in the fan.

As luck would have it, a major union (I forget which one, although CUPE represents Big Brothers and Big Sisters today) had just decided to try to unionize our office staff of one full-time and one part-time employee. The Executive Director was, of course, management and thus could not be unionized. There was no question in my mind at the time nor is there today that the union purposely targeted our fledging organization because of my involvement. I was no fan of unions and had made no bones about it on air. The union had decided to target social agencies, even those with only one or two employees, and Big Brothers is where they decided to start.

Now the union had a wonderful *cause célèbre*. Unfair labour practices, they screamed. "They fired the poor man because he supported unionization," was their claim. It blew up into a terrible storm. The entire School of Social Work at Carleton University attacked us with petitions and letters to the editors of both the *Ottawa Citizen* and the *Ottawa Journal*. The *Citizen* ran an editorial severely criticizing us and demanding that we explain the firing.

The problem was, everyone on the Board was afraid that if we even hinted at anything involving gay males, some mothers of boys who had already been matched might panic and Big Brothers would be plunged into a situation which it could not survive. We had also been alerted that some members of the gay community would pounce on us if we even whispered our reasons.

Rather foolishly, I suppose, I became so angry at what was happening that I publicly threatened to damn the torpedoes and tell the world exactly what had happened. When the union and others got wind of this, they immediately obtained a court injunction against our Board threatening all sorts of dire consequences if we dared say anything about the reasons for the firing.

Thus it was that we all had to endure several hours of screaming insults from a packed room during our annual meeting at the Château Laurier. We were called every name in the book by heaven only knows who. The worst part was that many of those screaming at us to give our reason for the firing knew bloody well our hands were tied. If we had revealed our reasons for firing our Executive Director, Big Brothers could not likely have survived and the Board itself would have faced very severe penalties. Some of those demanding that we tell all were involved in obtaining the injunction denying us the right to tell all! It was a terrible, sickening performance, believe me.

Reverend Norm Johnson had resigned from the Board in complete disgust earlier, and he went on to form Operation Go Home. I realized that I was a lightening rod so I stepped down as well, as did several other Board members who had had enough public flogging for a lifetime, thank you very much! Thank heavens some good solid people came forward, our punishment was not in vain, and somehow Big Brothers survived. Today I am very happy to say that Big Brothers has now amalgamated with Big Sisters (which I also helped to found) and is doing a marvelous and much needed job in our community with more than 160 matches.

I'm going to tell you something else that I have never told anyone before. Immediately following the highly critical and totally unfair editorial in the *Ottawa Citizen*, I contacted one of the editors. With assurances that what I was about to reveal was strictly off the record, I explained what was going on and asked if his paper couldn't do something to calm the storm because there was real danger Big Brothers would be destroyed. The editor sounded somewhat shocked and promised that the *Citizen* would "do something." He didn't explain what that "something" might be, but I was hoping for an editorial suggesting calm and that the Board's decision be respected. Sadly, the *Citizen* did absolutely nothing to clarify its editorial or try to help save Big Brothers.

That, of course, was a different time with different editors, different union leaders, and different students and professors. I can only hope that if a similar situation were to occur today, the treatment of a group of hard-working volunteers trying to improve the community would be somewhat less shameful.

The Flame

Pierre Berton called it "our last good year." I'm not certain of that, but there is no question that 1967, our centennial year, was a wonderful time to be a Canadian. Who can forget Expo 67, Man and His World, Bobby Gimby and "Can-a-da," "Ontario, a Place to Stand, A Place to Grow," and the Centennial Train's musical horn serenading us from coast to coast with "Oh Canada"?

Who can forget the incredible sense of pride and optimism? We were welcoming the world to the most spectacular world's fair in history, and our economy was booming. Special centennial projects sprang up across the country: civic centres, arenas, libraries, museums and art galleries. They named our first major league baseball team The Expos and Ottawa's first Junior A hockey team, the 67's. For a while at least, our usual Canadian reticence and fear of success was supplanted by a growing belief there was nothing we Canadians couldn't do if we put our minds to it. A sense of incredible achievement swept the land! Even the Americans were in awe!

The *Washington Post* ran an editorial, which said in part: "Canadians, whose ego, individualism and sense of personal worth have long suffered in the shadow of the colossus to the south will take a prideful look into the mirror and exclaim, 'WE DID IT!'"

As the old saying goes, what a difference a year makes.

Because, believe me, there was no sense of optimism in the land when I launched "The Greenline" in the summer of 1966. One of the first guests I had on the show was the indefatigable little Mayor of Montreal, Jean Drapeau, who was verbally pummelled by caller after caller.

"You're a crazy man, your islands will sink, you'll drive Montreal and Canada into the poorhouse, no one will come, your scheming will be an international embarrassment, it's a huge waste, it won't be done on time, we'll be the laughing stock of the world," more or less sums up a typical call that afternoon. A weaker or less determined man would surely have dissolved in a puddle of tears, or stormed out of the studio, but not Jean Drapeau. So charged was he with energy, good-will and excited optimism that to this day when I think of that abuse-ridden afternoon, I get a mental image of a little guy sitting there in front of the microphone with a shower of sparks flying off him. "Expo 67 will be the greatest world's fair the world has ever seen," he kept telling callers who usually responded with words of incredulity or snorts of derision.

I reminded him that the famous psychic Jeane Dixon had predicted that the islands he was building for Expo 67 in the St. Lawrence would sink before the year was out. "Is that so now?" he asked, "Jeane Dixon said that and she's an astrologer, is she?" pretending he hadn't been whacked over the head with the prediction countless times. "Well, let me tell you something—Napoleon Cadotte predicts that not only will the islands not sink but that Expo 67 will be the greatest world's fair in history!" I fell into the trap. "Who's Napoleon Cadotte?" He turned to me with a twinkle beneath those horn-rimmed glasses. "My gardener!"

It was pretty well the only laugh we had during the entire show.

The gardener, if in fact he existed, had no idea how right he was. Sixty-two nations took part in Expo 67. More than 50 million people—double the population of Canada in 1967—came to have a look and, with rare exception, fell in love with what they saw.

When Jean Drapeau made a surprise visit to my show on July 1, 1967, with Expo 67 at the height of its glory, several callers who just a year previously had called the Montreal mayor a fool and worse, managed to get through on our phone lines to apologize and thank him for what one woman, tears in her voice, said was the proudest time of her life.

As time began running out on that wonderful year, I was shocked to learn that one of the great symbols of our 100 years of confederation and of the centennial year itself was to be destroyed.

I was there on Parliament Hill as the Peace Tower clock struck that historic midnight hour and our 100th birthday was ushered in by Prime Minister Pearson lighting the newly completed Centennial Flame. As the flame sprang to life and fought bravely against the bitter wind, I broadcast the cheers of the thousands assembled there to a special network of listeners in more than 20 cities across the country.

But that was almost a year ago, and now the Secretary of State, Judy LaMarsh, the person responsible for centennial year, is telling us that the Centennial Flame, which has become a focal point for the tens of thousands of visitors to Parliament Hill, is going to be extinguished and the structure dismantled. When I object publicly, Ms. LaMarsh phones me personally to say that it was always the plan to extinguish the flame to mark the end of our great birthday party. "The Flame will be extinguished during a special ceremony at midnight on December 31," she informs me.

I go on the air the next day with the information, and the callers almost blow up the phone lines. "Look," says one young man, "this has been the greatest year in Canada's history, the government has done almost everything right for a change; please don't tell me that the very last act of our centennial year is going to be one of stupidity." I recall several callers saying that the Centennial Flame had become a symbol of our accomplishments, a constant reminder of how great we can be. We should keep it right there at the entrance to Parliament Hill for all time was the consensus.

And so I launch a major letter-writing campaign. Thousands of letters pour into the offices of Prime Minister Lester Pearson, Public Works Minister George McIlraith and Secretary of State Judy LaMarsh. More than 40,000 people sign a petition and this is before the Internet! After about a week of this, Ms. LaMarsh once again calls to tell me, off the record, that she agrees with my listeners and me but that the one who needs convincing is Works Minister McIlraith. "The Prime Minister," she says, "is sitting on the fence. He'll go along with whatever George decides."

The fact that it was Public Works Minister George McIlraith who seemed to be the fly in the ointment disturbed me greatly. Those of you who read *The Pork Chop and Other Stories* know that Mr. McIlraith and I tangled a couple of years earlier when I launched a campaign to assist

I was determined to use my influence and the power of my callers to ensure that the Centennial Flame, with which I am pictured above, would not be extinguished.

residents in the Metcalfe area obtain better phone service from the Metcalfe Phone Company, which was so poorly run it was stringing phone lines along fence posts in some areas. Unbeknownst to me at the time, Mr. McIlraith, as one of the owners of the Metcalfe Phone Company (even while Public Works Minister of Canada), put an arm twist on Kathleen Ryan, who was then owner of CFRA.

Together, they demanded that I retract what I was saying about his phone company. I refused and resigned, rather than deny what I knew to be true, but was persuaded to return a few days later when thousands of protests flooded into the station. The regulatory body of the day forced the sale of the Metcalfe Phone Company to Bell Canada, which undoubtedly cost Mr. McIlraith some money as well as prestige.

I decided to keep the pressure on to save the Flame in hopes that the Works Minister might remember what happened the last time he and I butted heads, so the next day I did some research and wrote the following editorial, which was broadcast on December 11, 1967, less than three weeks before the Flame was scheduled to be extinguished. It is one of only about a dozen editorials I wrote over a span of some 20 years at CFRA, which I have preserved because of their historical significance. I would take a bit more care with the writing if it were today, but that aside, here is the editorial that probably saved our Centennial Flame:

> The campaign to save the Centennial Flame appears to be paying off. We now have Mayor Reid, members of Council and a number of members of Parliament, along with thousands of Ottawa and area citizens anxious to save the Flame.

> The volume of mail to Works Minister McIlraith and Prime Minister Pearson from those in favor of retaining the structure has been extremely high.

There have been a great many figures kicked around as of late, concerning the cost of maintaining the Flame. Last week the Public Works Department informed me that the cost of keeping the Flame going would be about $3,000 a year, with some $3,500 worth of coins having been tossed into it, for a profit of about five hundred dollars.

In actual fact, the cost of running the Flame is about half the figure originally announced. For some reason, apparently, no one as yet has checked with Ottawa Gas on the cost—I did so this morning in an effort to see if the company could donate the gas. "We'd love to," a company official informed me, "but the Ontario Energy Board regulations do not allow for it. Just the same as Ontario Hydro would not be allowed to provide free hydro for some charitable purpose."

But General Manager Jack Spence says they have been able to work out an excellent rate for the government. Based on the volume of flow it will cost about $1,700 a year, not the $3,000 which was originally announced.

I'll repeat that. The cost of keeping the Flame going will be about $1,700 a year. There is no maintenance cost, as the men who care for the Parliamentary grounds tend the Flame as well. In other words, there are no extra men hired to look after it and no extra hours of overtime are required.

So quite obviously we can afford to keep the Flame going. If we want to be really cheap about it, we can take the coins from the fountain, pay the gas bill and turn over what's left to charity, or barring that we can pay out $1,700 a year, roughly what a government department would spend on paper clips for a few months.

As a matter of fact, if the Government really wants to be economy minded, leaving the Centennial Flame just where it is would be the cheapest thing to do. We've seen before what it costs to tear things down in this city.

But it still depends on you, whether the Flame is kept. A few more letters to the Works Minister may well turn the tide—to you we throw the torch!

• • •

Immediately after reading that editorial, I threw the phone lines open on "The Greenline" and was once again flooded with calls from people insisting, demanding, sometimes begging the Government to keep the Flame burning.

Exactly three days later, on December 14, 1967, Works Minister George McIlraith announced that the Government had decided to keep the Centennial Flame on Parliament Hill as a symbol of Canada's wonderful accomplishments during our first 100 years.

As you can see, back in 1967 the cost of keeping the flame burning seemed to be a very important issue. Considering the billions of dollars that poured out of government coffers for a plethora of centennial projects, it seems almost ludicrous today that the Flame might have been destroyed over two or three thousand dollars' upkeep a year. Especially when you consider that thousands of dollars' worth of coins are tossed into the Flame's liquid base each year, all of which is donated to various charities assisting the disabled.

The campaign to save the Centennial Flame was a very important landmark in the history of radio talk shows in Canada, or as we called them in the '60s and '70s, open-line shows. New and very important ground was broken. For the first time in Canada, a radio host used his audience as a lobby powerful enough to force even the federal government to change a policy. Don't forget, radio talk shows were in experimental infancy in this country when "The Greenline" was launched in 1966, and for the most part they were intended as nothing but pure entertainment aimed primarily at housewives. There were only a small handful of shows in the entire country, almost all of them devoted to what we today call lifestyle issues. You know the kind of thing I'm talking about: Should men have to help their wives in the kitchen? What do you think of the latest Hollywood romance? That kind of fuzzy stuff. The idea that a single radio host could wield sufficient influence or power, if you

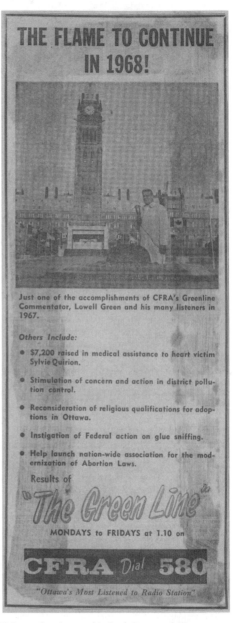

CFRA ran the above ad in both Ottawa dailies on December 30, 1967. The show was definitely gaining influence!

like, to get a government at any level to change direction was an eye-opener for me and anyone in broadcasting who was paying attention.

It is true that Jack Webster on the west coast had begun to move beyond the Hollywood "fluff stuff" and was hammering the BC Government on various issues, but for the most part, his was a guest-driven show, which kept listeners as spectators rather than active participants.

It is with pride that I say the concept of creating an active constituency involved not just in listening or calling but in carrying out various campaigns, either to lobby government or as a fund-contributing arm, began with "The Greenline's" listeners' successful efforts to save the Centennial Flame.

Until then, talk shows such as "The Greenline" were considered by many to be a kind of "freak show," attracting only the very elderly, so desperately lonely they would listen to anything, or the desperately dumb. The truth of the matter is, of course, that well-run talk shows dealing with important issues of the day attract a very loyal audience of well-educated people of all ages and incomes who are interested in and concerned about the world around them.

If you don't care what the Mayor, the Prime Minister or the world are up to, you aren't listening to "The Lowell Green Show." And if you dare call me, you'd at the very least better know where the St. Lawrence Seaway is!

Helping Santa

"You know something that I think is really disgraceful, Lowell?" I'm quick on the uptake. "Let me guess. The government?" The caller, whose name I have long since forgotten chuckles a bit. "Well that too, but no, that's not what I'm calling about. It's the fact that here we are two years past our centennial, and Ottawa, the capital of the country, doesn't even have a Santa Claus Parade. Toronto keeps boasting about having had a Santa Claus Parade for almost a hundred years. My kids are always glued to the TV when they televise it, but I just can't believe we don't have a parade here in Ottawa. What's the matter with us here, anyway?"

It's a good question, for which I have no answer, but like a darn fool I come up with one anyway. "Know what?" I say. "You're absolutely right. I'm going to start one!"

Little did I know what I was getting myself in for. The fateful call was made in late October 1969. If I was really going to get a parade started, I was going to have to saddle up and get riding mighty fast.

As luck would have it, that evening we had a meeting of the Bank Street Merchant's Association of which, as owner of the Little Farm Pet Shop on Bank Street, I was not only a member but also the president. The merchants, to their credit, were enthused at the idea but doubted we had time to properly organize a parade for that year. Knowing full well how quickly good ideas can die, I continued to push the merchants and foolishly offered to organize it myself. It was then that one of the members at the meeting, whose name I am sorry to say I have forgotten, made a brilliant suggestion. "You know," she said, "it might be a good idea if instead of having Santa throwing candy and other stuff into the crowd, we had the crowd bring presents to Santa which we could then hand out to some of the less fortunate kids in our city." How could anyone say no to that?

And that's how our very unique Help Santa Claus Parade started. I went on the air the next day and met with tremendous enthusiasm from all callers, some of whom volunteered or suggested various marching bands, majorette troops, floats, displays, and so on. City Councillor Charlie St. Germain, who had assisted Santa on many occasions in the past, and had a wonderful hearty laugh, volunteered to don the red suit. We were off to the races.

What landed on my desk was a logistical nightmare. Marching bands we contacted warned that if the temperature dropped too low on parade day, many of their instruments would freeze up. Various parents of majorette troops raised hell if their daughter wasn't able to march to a particular band. The bands themselves, if they were able to play, had to be spaced so their sounds would not intermingle. There were disputes about the route. Some merchants, incredibly, didn't want it on their street. One particular ethnic group, which had prepared a rather dramatic float, dropped out at the last minute when they learned another ethnic group was taking part. We got into a wrangle over where toys and money collected should be donated. I had a promise from a Montreal firm that they would loan us the use of a hovercraft for Santa to ride in but city officials put the kibosh on that for fear of blowing dust and stones. The Humane Society protested at the idea of a team of huskies pulling a sled on rollers, and so it went. It wasn't long until I was ready to pull my hair out. Never again, I promised myself, will I ever volunteer for anything!

I've never believed in miracles, but something approaching a miracle happened on parade day. The weather was a couple degrees above freezing, warm enough for the bands; the crowds were large, very appreciative and very generous. I can't say it went off without a hitch, but as my Uncle Bill used to say, "By gum and by George, we got her done!"

And then I realized I had another problem. Not only had I not arranged to transport the toys from the parade to a storage location, but I hadn't arranged a storage location! For some reason, it had never dawned on me that some people would actually come to the parade with gifts.

From somewhere, my buddy Paul (Punchy) Lapointe, who had worked with me diligently all day, rounded up a half-ton truck into which we loaded well over a thousand toys. "Now what do we do with them?" he asked.

The only place I could think of that was large enough was the main floor studio at CFRA on Isabella Street. I managed to get a window open and we started unloading.

What I didn't know was that Joe Brown and the Happy Wanderers, one of the most popular bands ever to play the Ottawa Valley, had booked the studio for a recording session the next day.

You know what happened. With toys piled waist-high against it, there was no way they could get the door open. Not in the least amused, Joe sent a couple of Wanderers with good backs through the window; they cleared the door and a small space in the middle and managed somehow to finish their recording session with Joe swearing revenge.

The next day we shipped all the toys and a considerable amount of money off to the Rideau Regional Institute in Smiths Falls. They were delighted, and I managed to steer clear of Joe Brown until he cooled down a bit. I shouldn't have worried. When he learned what it was all about, Joe took up a collection from the band members and added it to the total after extracting a promise from me that I'd find a different storage area next year.

Organizing a parade of that size was just too much for one person, however, so next year the Ottawa Fire Department volunteered to take over and has been doing a wonderful job since. As far as I can determine, it is still the only Santa Claus Parade in Canada, maybe in the world, where people bring toys to Santa, not the other way around. And that seems to me to be the true spirit of Christmas!

Bless My Buttons!

One of my best buddies has a son who swears up and down to this day that he once talked with the real Santa Claus. He's almost right. Bernie McManus, God rest his soul, was as close to the real Santa Claus as we're ever likely to get.

Bernie was a well known and much loved local actor, who on Christmas Eve for more than ten years enthralled children and adults alike with his portrayal of Santa on undoubtedly the most popular call-in show I ever hosted. Hands up all of you who remember his famous, "WELL, BLESS MY BUTTONS!" Honestly now, did anyone ever do it better?

I've talked with parents and even grandparents today who tell me that as four-, five- and six-year-olds they trembled with excitement waiting on the line to tell Santa what they wanted for Christmas. One of those parents is my own daughter, Lianne, who as a four-year-old became so excited when Santa finally came on the line to talk with her that she…

well, I'd better not embarrass her since she now has a five-year-old of her own who would think what her mommy did was mighty hilarious!

Bernie took his two-hour stint as Santa so seriously that I've often

Bless my buttons! Local actor and swell guy Bernie McManus was by far the most popular guest I ever had. His Santa Claus enthralled kids and adults alike for years. If there was a single person within sound of our voices who didn't listen to our special Christmas Eve broadcasts during those years, I would be very surprised.

wondered if the strain of that show helped to shorten his life. He would arrive in the station at least two hours prior to broadcast, loaded down with little notes to himself, letters and sometimes pictures spilling from his pockets. He was always very worried if it was okay to bring his famous set of sleigh bells, by this time squashed, dented and rusty, but the most melodious I've ever heard. In later shows, he brought along a little plastic block and a toy hammer. The block, he claimed, was a magic screen which when "pinged" with the hammer, allowed him to actually see the little boy or girl who was calling. This was indeed a marvelous invention, but one that sometimes caused us considerable grief.

Kids are not dumb, as you know, so as soon as they knew Santa could actually see them they often would ask the jolly old fellow what he thought of their new haircut, or the black eye their brother had recently administered. One young lass even went so far as to inquire of Santa if he thought her mommy was getting too fat. Daddy apparently had been complaining!

One year my good buddy Paul Niebergall came to me to ask a favour. His five-year-old son, Jamie, was beginning to have some serious doubts about the existence of Santa. "He's bound and determined to call the show tomorrow," said Paul, "but I'm a bit worried he may ask some very embarrassing questions. Think you can bring the kid around?"

No problem. I prepped Santa a bit, and sure enough, about an hour into the show, comes the call from our little buddy, Jamie. "Are you really…," he begins to ask, but Bernie is ready for him and fires off all barrels. "Jamie, little Jamie out there in Kanata. Now, I know you very well. Why old Santa saw you trying to hit some golf balls onto the golf course just behind your house a couple of weeks ago and you almost hit a window. Now, Jamie, you weren't really supposed to do that, were you?" Jamie is thunderstruck. There's dead silence at the other end of the line. Bernie continues, "BUT BLESS MY BUTTONS, JAMIE," you've been so good to your dog Ginger that old Santa will have some wonderful toys under the tree for you, don't you worry now, but remember, no more golf balls." There's only a tiny squeak at the other end of the line, and then a whispered, "Thank you, Santa."

Bernie was just as wonderfully adept at fielding little minefield questions that often popped up as he was at teasing me for my terrible gaffs. I was forever putting my foot into it by suggesting such things as leaving hay out for the reindeer, or maybe spiking Santa's milk with something from Daddy's locked cabinet. By the end of the show, Bernie and I often had tears pouring down our cheeks from laughter. The show actually was carried out on two levels—one for the kids, the other for their parents. Especially popular was Santa's yearly present to me of a big chunk of coal for being such a "bad boy" all year long.

In later years, Bernie began having difficulty remembering names and I could see that the strain was taking a toll on him. I suggested that perhaps we could retire him for a younger version, but right up until the end he just wouldn't hear of it.

There is no question that Bernie McManus was one of the most beloved characters who ever appeared on CFRA, and judging by the queries I receive wherever I go, BLESS MY BUTTONS, one of the most missed, as well.

The Car Thief

I've finally got one! In all her glory. A 1972, almost brand spanking new Lincoln Continental. Plum coloured, inside and out. Half the size of a football field. All fenders, chrome and glitz. The kid from the farm has come a long way, baby! From shearing sheep, to toast of the town and the automobile to prove it. It's great to be alive. Married to a beautiful woman, two great kids, half the city listening in to "The Greenline" every day, and now finally, I've traded in the drafty old Jeep for a Lincoln—A LINCOLN, for heaven's sake! Only a few thousand miles on her, hardly a scratch, and gasoline only about 40 cents a gallon!

Except, wait just a minute. It *was* there! Where the heck has it gone? I'm beside myself with shock and anger. Dashing into the CFRA studio at 150 Isabella Street, I signal to afternoon host Trevor Kidd that I've got some vital information I must pass on to his listeners. Sensing some really interesting stuff, Trevor signals me towards the mic and indicates it's all mine. "Trevor," I say, slightly out of breath, "I can't believe this. I pulled my car into our parking lot behind our building here about ten minutes ago, left the motor running while I rushed in for some things I forgot, and when I went back outside—can you believe it? SOMEONE HAS STOLEN MY CAR! TREVOR, SOMEONE HAS STOLEN MY CAR RIGHT OUT OF OUR PARKING LOT HERE AT CFRA."

Trevor is shaking his head partly, I suspect, at the audacity of the thief, partly at my stupidity for parking a car with its motor running.

I describe the missing car and ask listeners to be on the lookout for it, never imagining for a moment what was about to happen.

I am no sooner out of the studio when the switchboard operator pages me. "Lowell," she whispers when I pick up the phone, "I've got a guy here on the line who says he's got your car. Claims he's the guy who stole it, and says he's really sorry, he didn't know it was yours and wants to return it to you."

I don't believe a word of it, but on the off chance it's not some kook trying to be funny, the call is patched through to me. It's a young-sounding guy, tripping over himself with apologies. "Geez, Mr. Green," he says, "I didn't know the car was yours. I'm a big fan. I'm really sorry, if I had known it was yours I would never have taken it."

"Where the hell are you?" I ask. There's a brief pause. "About halfway to Hawkesbury. Look, I'm going to turn around right now and bring it back. I don't want you or the cops there to greet me, so give me a number where I can call you and tell you where I've left it." Not really believing this is happening, I nonetheless give him my office number and sit down to wait with a heap of doubt and a smidgen of hope.

Believe it or not, about an hour later my phone rings. It's the Lincoln thief. "Okay," he says, "I left it in the parking lot at the Talisman Motor Inn on Carling Avenue." He pauses for a second and then in a kind of wistful voice, says, "You know, I could have gotten two thousand bucks for that car if I had just left it at Jean Talon and St-Denis in Montreal!" I'm not sure what he expects, but I'm in no mood to suggest any kind of reward. I do manage a "Thanks," hang up and rush out to pick up my car before this character changes his mind.

Now fast-forward about five years. I get a phone call from a friend of mine on the Ottawa Police Force. "Lowell," he asks, "do you know a guy named...?"—and here he mentions a name that means absolutely nothing to me and I have long since forgotten. "Never heard of him," I reply. "Why?"

"Well," says the cop, "I just arrested this guy for breaking into a lumberyard and he claims he's a friend of yours who once found your missing car!"

It dawns on me and I burst into laughter. "Yeah, he returned my car all right. After he stole it! Why did he give you my name?"

There's a chuckle at the other end of the line. "Don't really know, but I guess this guy wants you to give him a good character reference!"

We both explode in laughter. I have no idea what happened to our friend. Either he gave up stealing for a living, or decided against using me as a reference, because I never heard from him again.

The Lincoln, as it turned out, was a bit of a lemon and used to stall at the most inopportune times. Maybe it was the colour! I got rid of it a few months after its rescue, traded her in on a Chevy. Blue. Really more my style and not worth nearly as much, I suspect, parked at Jean Talon and St-Denis!

T. K.

Frank Ryan is on the tear again! This time CFRA Sales Manager George Gowling is on the listening end of things. "Listen to this, George. I distinctly told him I didn't want him going to Detroit this week," rants Frank as he turns up the monitor in his office. There is no mistaking the sonorous voice of Terry Kielty booming over the sound of an excited crowd.

"Tigers are trailing by three here in the bottom of the sixth, two out, Al Kaline dances off the bag at third…the count is three and two on Norm Cash…heerrrre comes the pitch…"

Angrily, Frank snaps off the monitor. "Who the hell does Terry think owns this station, him or me? I'm the one paying the damn bills around here and if I've told him once I've told him a dozen times those trips to Detroit are costing us too much." Frank is working himself into a full-blown froth. "He knows bloody well that unless it's a doubleheader I want him to stay in Ottawa and do a reconstruction.

Besides which, George, there's not a single one of your clients who can tell whether Terry's doing the broadcast from here or Detroit. In fact, I had a guy from Myers Motors tell me yesterday he thinks Terry's reconstruction's are better than the real thing."

Frank, who's been known to let his Irish temper get the better of him from time to time, slams his fist down on his desk. "George, if he won't listen to the guy who owns the station, maybe he'll listen to you. You deal with it!"

George is a bit puzzled. "You know," he says slowly, "I swear I saw Terry no more than two hours ago—how the hell could he get to Tiger Stadium so fast?"

Frank Ryan looks at George Gowling. George Gowling looks at Frank Ryan. Without a word, both dart out the door, up a flight of stairs, down a hall and into master control just as an excited Terry Kielty shouts, "Here comes the throw to the plate...SAFE!" The crowd noise rocks the studio where Terry, not yet having seen Frank and George, pumps his fist in the air. He's obviously a Tigers fan!

Wait a minute, I can almost hear you say. Terry Kielty is broadcasting a Detroit Tigers game from the CFRA studios?! That's right. What's more, he's so good at it, not even the guy who signs his paycheque can tell that Terry's not in Detroit doing play-by-play in the midst of a roaring crowd only a few yards from the playing field!

Frank and George look at each other sheepishly. Frank gives a feeble thumbs-up to Terry and heads downstairs, admitting afterwards he's laughing at himself and shaking his head in wonder.

So how did Terry do it and make it sound so real? Well, it wasn't easy. The only way for Terry to follow the game in those days is with the aid of a small teleprinter set up near the microphone. The tape keeps him informed, more or less, with what is going on, pitch by pitch, utilizing a kind of made-up code.

Terry is provided the lineups and batting order for the day in advance of the game. Each player is assigned two initials. Norm Cash is N.C. Eddie Yost is E.Y. You get the picture. That isn't a problem. When it comes to calling balls and strikes—that can be a problem because the tickertape also gives the pitch location. Thus, the tape would read, let's say, N.C. B 1 O—to which Terry Kielty would say something like…and now Norm Cash steps up to the plate, batting 325—3rd in the American league. Norm had two hits in yesterday's game, although he's always had difficulty in the past against 39-year-old Early Wynn (pause) Wynn looks in for the sign. Here comes the pitch—ball one outside. The tape now reads B 2 L—to which Terry might say…Cash steps back from the plate readjusts his hat, steps in again—here comes the pitch—ball two low this time (pause) Wynn steps off the mound—fingers the rosin bag—steps back on the mound—looks in again for the sign. The tape now reads S 1 O C—so Terry says strike on the outside corner—the count is now two balls one strike (pause) Cash steps back from the plate—takes a couple practice swings—he's ready—steps back into the box. The machine spits out H C 1—Terry immediately gives the microphone a sharp rap with his pencil—gives a signal to his operator in master control to jack up the crowd noise and says in an excited voice—It's a hit—just over the second baseman's head into centre field—Cash rounds first—comes diving back, just in time to beat the throw from centre field…and so on.

As you can see, a little invention is required—a little creativity. No doubt, if anyone happened to be watching the game on television while listening to Terry Kielty, they would be more than a little puzzled! The crowd noise on Terry's broadcast is about three minutes of an endless loop of tape that I doubt very much was even recorded in Tiger Stadium. If you listen very carefully, you can hear the same hot-dog vendor call out every three minutes.

The operator has done this so many times he can usually adjust the sound up or down simply by listening to the inflection in Terry's voice.

One of the problems with the machine is that frequently it sends garbled code or stops working for a minute or two. Terry is a master at covering up for these delays. Listen to one of Terry's reconstructed broadcasts and you were likely to hear wonderful entertaining stories about dogs running onto the field, fans falling out of the stands, or winds whipping up dust and the umpire calling time out to remove dirt from his eyes. There was no one better at it than Terry Kielty, and Frank Ryan was correct when he said that very often Terry's reconstructed games done from the studio were more exciting than the ones done from the stadium.

There was another big advantage to doing broadcasts from the studio rather than the ancient, drafty toilet-challenged broadcast booth at Tiger Stadium. At CFRA when the urge hit you, you simply told your audience that police were chasing a fan across the field, or there was a slight rain delay or something, slapped on a few commercials, and then took a little stroll down the hall. Presto, there you were—a modern, convenient, honest-to-goodness flush toilet. At Tiger Stadium, on the other hand, it was no little stroll but rather a long hike down a shaky ladder to get in line with a few hundred beer-guzzling auto workers. At Tiger Stadium only the very unwise didn't forgo liquids for several hours prior to the game and make sure everything was well drained before the ascent to the broadcast booth.

That would work fairly well for the properly prepared during a regular nine-inning game. It got a little dicey if it went into two or three extra innings, but there aren't many of us able to hold out for a seven-hour 22-inning game!

It's June 24, 1962—a day in baseball broadcaster infamy. At least it is for Jim Shearon who has taken over play-by-play duties from

Terry Kielty who had assumed more responsibilities as General Manager of CFRA.

The Yankees, who would go on to win the World Series that year, were in Detroit to play the Tigers. Jim had dutifully performed all his customary ablutions prior to the game, clambered up the ladder to the booth and, for nine full innings, painted a graphic verbal picture of a classic struggle between two of the finest baseball teams in the world. On the field were some of baseball's most famous names: Mickey Mantle, Roger Marris, Yogi Berra for New York; Al Kaline, Norm Cash, Jim Bunning for Detroit.

As befitting a clash of titans, the score was tied at the end of nine innings—and at the end of ten. No change after 11 or 12 or 13. By this time Jim is getting desperate. Even more so by the end of 15, and then 16, at which point he spots an empty Coke bottle lying on the floor of the booth. I won't be more descriptive than that.

Jim had no way of knowing it at the time (frankly he had other worries on his mind) but by the time Jack Reed hit a home run in the 22nd inning to win it 9–7 for the Yankees, Jim Shearon had just broadcast the longest baseball game in the history of the major leagues. More than seven hours in all, and just to add a bit of drama…that home run that relief pitcher Jack Reed hit? It was the only home run he ever hit in the 222 games in which he appeared!

Of course, the big question is, what in the world was an Ottawa radio station doing broadcasting Detroit Tiger baseball games? The answer is quite simple. Most Canadian radio stations, including CFRA in Ottawa, really didn't understand radio in those days and essentially were flying by the seat of their pants with no real clue as to what it was they were doing. Let me explain.

The Evolution

When I started in Brantford in 1956, FM radio had been invented but wouldn't actually be launched for another four or five years. Most small to mid-sized towns had only two radio stations—a CBC affiliate and one privately owned station. Both naturally broadcast on the AM band. Larger cities, such as Ottawa, might have two, possibly three private stations along with a CBC outlet. Even in cities such as Toronto and Montreal you could count the number of private radio stations on the fingers of one hand until the mid-1960s, all of them scrambling to find out if video really had killed the radio star, in other words, was there life after the advent of television.

In most cases when I arrived in Ottawa in 1960, programming was all over the map. With the exception of CHUM in Toronto, which launched "Top 40" radio in 1957 aimed almost exclusively at the under-25 demographic, most programmers were still trying to be all things to all people well into the '60s. I use the word programmers loosely, since in most stations, the idea of programming was to have the various DJs pick their favourite records to play and to say whatever popped into their heads.

This would usually be mixed in with news and sports coverage and whatever else the owner or manager or DJ chose. In CFRA's case this meant a great deal of farm broadcasting and coverage of some Detroit Tigers baseball games—either live from Tiger Stadium or reconstructed by Terry Kielty.

Just to further confuse listeners, announcers, newscasters and DJs tended to move in and out of markets very rapidly, each new one bringing a different idea of what constituted "good programming."

In the space of about four months in the early 1960s, CFRA's morning show went from Les Lye and his alter ego Abercrombie featuring clever humour and middle-of-the-road music, to a guy who played rock and roll, followed almost immediately by a former CBC announcer who played, believe it or not, classical music. You can imagine what a great way that was to build a loyal audience!

Not only was programming likely to change very rapidly in any given time slot, but it changed drastically from time slot to time slot.

In those early days, CHUM in Toronto seemed to be about the only radio station in the country that was able to wrap its mind around the fact that to be successful, radio should try to keep listeners tuned in as long as possible, and that the only way to do that was to choose the demographic you wanted to attract to your station, then program only what that demographic wanted to listen to. CHUM played Top 40 music 24 hours a day hosted by wacky, fast-talking announcers. So young people who wanted to listen to Top 40, delivered by wacky, fast-talking announcers knew exactly where to find it. Furthermore, they could listen all day long because there was nothing on the station they didn't want to hear.

Programming that would feature a rock song one minute, classical music the next, followed by an hour of farm news, followed by a three- or four-hour baseball game, followed by whatever appealed to the announcer on duty might gain you a reasonable number of listeners when there was very little competition in the marketplace. This was especially true when the competition was doing the same thing, but as more and more radio stations sprang up, successful stations were forced to take a page from CHUM Toronto's book and they began to tailor their programming for one specific demographic. As more and more stations came on stream, the demographic became more and more specific.

I don't want to get too technical here, but to give you a rough idea what I'm talking about—in the late '60s and right into the '80s, a radio station might target housewives in general during the afternoon. But when you awoke one morning to find that there were ten or fifteen stations all after the same audience and, furthermore, that your housewife audience had largely morphed into men and women in the workplace, you had to narrow your focus and program for one small segment of that audience. The more stations competing with you, the narrower the focus had to be until, today, you have a radio station programming for just about every kind of demographic you can imagine: Oldies radio for older people who like nostalgia in their music; Bob-FM for younger working women; Majic for older working women; CFRA for older males; The Team for younger males; Chez for middle-aged males; The Bear for slightly younger males, but not into the Team's sports or raunch, and so it goes. Religious radio for the religious, ethnic radio for ethnic minorities.

There is a joke that has been making the rounds in radio for some time that says if you want to target women aged 24, five-foot-two with eyes of blue, wearing red shoes, there's a station aimed directly at them!

Name a demographic, French or English, Ottawa today has some 27 radio stations each aimed primarily at a well-defined, specific segment of the population. There is always some spill over. Not all working women over the age of 30 listen to Majic (thank heaven for that!). Talk radio is aimed primarily at men over the age of 35, but CFRA has strong listenership in almost all demographics. In each case, if the programmers are doing their job properly, the majority of each station's audience will be in the demographic it programs for.

When I arrived in radio, the various announcers or DJs picked their own music so there was no continuity, no understanding even of the audience they were trying to attract. Today, no successful radio station will play a single record without first having it listened to and approved by a focus group of their targeted demographic. If you program for women aged 35 to 60, then everything you hear on that station will have first been listened to and approved by a group of women in that age group. In today's fast-paced world, play one song your audience doesn't like and you can almost hear thousands of radio dials being punched off, or onto a competitor.

I'm going to let you in on a trade secret here. It's not all that different with talk radio. Don't get me wrong, no talk-show host worth his or her salt would ever let management or sponsors dictate what they say, but the owners, station managers and program directors do get to choose the demographic they wish to reach and the host they believe is best suited to reach that particular group of people.

Radio talk shows, as a general rule, appeal to an older demographic, traditionally skewed roughly 60 percent male to 40 percent female—but if station management has reason to believe there is a better opportunity to attract a younger, or more female-dominated audience, this may be accomplished by conducting a "lifestyle" issues program rather than one dealing with current events or politics. A younger host may also assist in attracting a younger audience, although interestingly enough, this is not always the case. For the most part, it is the issues chosen for discussion that dictate the demographic that listens. Proper positioning of topics may also encourage more women to listen.

What is key, just as with music programming, is that whatever format is chosen for the talk show, it must be consistent. The show dealing mainly with civic affairs and politics must not stray far from that. Ditto the one dealing with lifestyles. The left-wing host must in every case remain left-wing on all issues. It goes without saying the right-wing host must also remain true to those political leanings on all topics. I, for example, am opposed to the death penalty, but because I know the majority of my listeners support the death penalty, I do my utmost to stay away from that topic. One thing you must never do is lie about your feelings; your listeners will pick up on it every time! Another topic I stay away from is abortion, since whatever position I take is bound to really tick off a large group of people. Forget your win-win situation. Abortion is a lose-lose topic if ever there was one, and believe me, I'm not in radio to lose!

Fans of rock music will the turn the radio off if they hear classical. Fans of right-wing talk will turn the radio off if they hear left-wing. And so it goes.

It is amazing to me the number of radio hosts and even station managers who don't understand that.

I'll tell you what else amazes me, and that is why some Ottawa radio stations, I'm thinking particularly here of Oldies 1310 (formerly CKOY), don't launch a lifestyles talk format aimed at attracting younger listeners, especially younger women. It would cut into CFRA's listenership to some small degree, but in my opinion the Ottawa market is wide open for some lighter talk programming. The major drawback with talk, of course, is the high cost. Hiring competent hosts and support staff doesn't come cheap. "Spinning" music is undoubtedly far less expensive, but in the end, if done properly, talk can be highly profitable. It certainly is for CFRA, which is one of the most profitable radio stations in Canada, despite the salaries of guys like Steve Madely and Lowell Green, who don't come cheap.

But, like it or not, there is a huge market for so-called "soft talk," or lifestyle talk as I describe it. All you have to do is think about the media coverage of, and the obvious interest in, every breath that Britney Spears or Paris Hilton take. In that regard, remember the endless coverage given to the death and subsequent court battles involving Anna Nicole Smith? You can complain all you like about the dumbing down of

Canada, but let's be very honest here, the only reason the media gives such heavy play to stories about movie stars and their love lives and excesses is because there is a segment of the audience that soaks up that kind of stuff. Those people buy products too!

What's important to remember, however, is that when "soft talk"— that is, lifestyles, fashions and celebrity-obsession programming—is confronted with well-done hard talk, the station programming hard talk will win every time. It would be very difficult to dislodge CFRA's position in the marketplace, and no sane programmer would even try, but there is still, in my opinion, a wide open market for "soft talk" in Ottawa. But what the heck do I know?

What I did know when I came back from Toronto to host "The Lowell Green Show" on CFRA in Ottawa, was that I wanted to build a take-no-prisoners, small "c" conservative show. For five years I had watched as CFRB Toronto allowed its huge audience to dissipate as the station switched more and more from hard-hitting, current events-driven talk to lifestyle "soft talk." When I started at CFRB in the early '90s, it boasted that it was the most listened to radio station in Canada, no small feat for an AM radio station. When I left to come to Ottawa in 1994, it was still the top-rated station in Toronto, but you could see the tide shifting as management slipped further and further into lifestyles programming with such shows as the husband and wife team of "The Motts" in the afternoon. Today, CFRB is a long way from the top-rated station in Toronto, let alone in Canada, thanks to, in the opinion of many, management that just doesn't understand the dynamics of talk radio.

It convinced me more than ever that a hard-hitting talk show in Ottawa would be a big winner, and as increasingly I was becoming more conservative minded, it was only natural for me to take the path on which I could be totally honest. But launching a right-wing, or small "c" conservative, talk show in Ottawa was a very tough job, believe me, in an essentially Liberal and NDP city.

The first couple of ratings, to put it bluntly, weren't all that hot, as most of our Liberal and NDP listeners hated me and turned their radios off. The complaints flooded in. Fortunately, we had intelligent management that understood what was happening, and gradually, as more and more conservative-minded listeners found the show, our audience began to build, until today it is by far the most listened to show in Ottawa and the Valley in its time period. In some of the most recent ratings, about 30 percent of listeners over the age of 35 are tuned in to "The Lowell Green Show." This in a city with 27 radio stations and more than 20 percent of potential listeners really unavailable because of an inability to understand English very well.

One of the fascinating things about talk radio all across North America is that, almost without exception, the top-rated shows are all conservative, the most notable of which in Canada is "The Lowell Green Show," and in the United States is Rush Limbaugh's show.

There is a reason for this. Most of the mainstream media in both Canada and the United States are well to the left of the political spectrum. Many ordinary citizens who have conservative leanings have long felt that their points of view have not been well represented, so when a conservative voice such as that of Rush or Lowell comes along it helps to validate their beliefs. You can almost hear some listeners say with tremendous relief: Thank God, you feel that way too. I thought I was the only one! The media, from radio and television to newspapers and magazines, are filled with left-wing ideology. Only on a handful of radio programs can you hear the other side of the story.

Talk radio, of course, rescued AM radio. In fact, talk was largely invented to save AM radio, which just cannot compete for quality of sound with FM. With music radio, FM is going to win every time because music just sounds better on the FM band than on AM. Thus has evolved talk radio of every conceivable type—news-talk, sports-talk, religion-talk, health-talk, car-talk...all with one common thread: talk not music.

A few AM stations are still bobbing along with various types of music formats, most of them just barely keeping their head above financial water. Many AM stations have simply shut down, including CBC AM in Ottawa and an AM station in Hull. In the United States, most AM stations have become little more than relay outposts with almost all programming coming from one central location and perhaps the odd bit of local weather or news thrown in. Only those AM stations that have had the wisdom (and the money) to hire intelligent, well-read, entertaining hosts with well-defined ideologies succeed with talk.

It is my belief, and there is plenty of evidence to support this, that the stations that do best at talk are those that have hosts taking strong stands on issues featured on the front pages of the daily newspapers. Lifestyle topics and Hollywood happenings won't prompt as many complaints to the CRTC, but the shows and the stations that really do well are those that are so forceful and current even your enemies are afraid not to listen!

The stations that do the best are those that matter, by that I mean have influence in the community. And the only way a radio station is going to matter, is if a host with influence weighs in on issues that matter to its listeners.

The big winners in all of this are the advertisers. Once again, let me explain why.

Because each radio station has such a well-defined demographic listenership, it makes it very cost efficient for advertisers to reach potential customers. One of the big problems with advertising in daily newspapers is that the guy selling jeans to teens has to pay for readers who are only interested in retirement homes or Cadillacs. The retirement home advertiser must pay for readers only interested in buying jeans. Newspapers base their lineage rates on the total number of readers, including those who have no interest in your product.

Radio, on the other hand, allows the advertiser to directly target those he believes are his most likely clients. The store selling sneakers to teens can pick a station or two whose audiences are comprised primarily of teens. The mountain bike store can pick the station or stations catering to young active males. These days, radio stations are so sophisticated they can tell you the average incomes and education of their listeners, so that the guy selling Cadillacs knows exactly where to get the best bang for his buck. How frequently his potential customers will hear the message is also a very important consideration. There is an old saying in radio that frequency sells. That's true but only if those listening are really potential customers. The best examples of this are the various "Experts on Call" programs many stations now carry. These are strictly hour-long infomercials for which the client pays very handsomely despite these programs usually having very small audiences.

The reason clients are prepared to pay as much as they do is that while there may be only a few thousand people listening to a particular "expert," those who are listening have a direct interest in whatever is being sold. Far better to have a thousand potential customers listening, than ten thousand who have no interest whatsoever in what you are trying to sell.

This increasing specialization, the narrowing of demographics, the ability of advertisers to hone in with great frequency on those in the age and income bracket interested and able to buy their products, are the main reasons radio has been able to survive, thrive even, despite the tremendous competition from television, newspapers, direct mail, and the Internet.

The role satellite radio will play in all of this remains to be seen, but here's something else I know for sure. While there is a market for all formats—music, talk or whatever—in radio, well-executed local programming will always win. This is especially true in Canada. For about a year we tried syndicating "The Lowell Green Show" to several cities across the country. At one point we were being broadcast in Halifax, Windsor, Sudbury, Peterborough, Montreal and Winnipeg, as well as Ottawa, but it just didn't work well enough. People want local programming.

The most drastic negative effect was right here in Ottawa. It was obvious people in Montreal had no interest in what Ottawa City Council was doing; Winnipeg couldn't care less about Montreal's language problems; and Halifax wasn't really interested in anything other than what occurred in the Atlantic provinces.

Perhaps the most graphic example of this lack of interest in national affairs was demonstrated on October 31, 1995, when I broadcast live from the heart of Ste-Catherine Street in Montreal as Quebeckers went to the polls in a referendum to decide the fate of our country. It was one of the finest broadcasts I have ever done. Separatists and federalists joined us to state their case and make predictions. We had interviews with many leading Canadians, including the Prime Minister, and the premiers of several provinces. Callers were passionate on both sides. We were able to confirm that, indeed, many Quebec banks had made preparations to ship assets out of the province in the event of a separatist victory. A spokesman for the Crees of Northern Quebec called from the far north to state emphatically that they were prepared to take up arms in order to remain within Canada. The broadcast even featured a spontaneous near fist fight on air between a separatist and a federalist, both of whom were nonetheless able to state their positions eloquently.

The show won many broadcast awards and nominations, but believe it or not, most of the stations aside from Ottawa and Montreal received dozens of complaints. To sum up, listeners in places like Halifax, Windsor, Sudbury, Peterborough and Winnipeg made it very clear they couldn't care less what happened in Quebec, even if it led to a shooting war. They wanted local programming.

As a consequence, in order to satisfy all our various clients, we had to almost completely ignore local news, which as you might suspect began to dampen our ratings in Ottawa. Imagine a talk show in Ottawa where we would deny callers the opportunity to discuss hot local issues, such as light rail or the election of Larry O'Brien as Mayor. Ditto major local stories in other cities.

You can understand why we decided to end syndication and concentrate more on local issues. It's my belief, however, that with the right host, a syndicated one-hour evening show dealing with national and international issues could attract a respectable following across the country, but that it would not be strong enough to justify air time during the prime daytime hours. Would I like to do it? I'd love to!

To boil it all down, the ability of advertisers to target their market with radio is the reason video didn't kill the radio star. In fact, while well-programmed radio stations continue to attract larger and larger audiences, despite ever-increasing competition, newspapers, especially broadsheet newspapers, are facing declining readership almost everywhere.

The Expos and Me

Did I play any kind of role in bringing the Expos to Montreal? I don't know for sure, but the fact is, I may have! You be the judge. First, let's back up a bit.

Montreal was awarded a National League Baseball franchise on May 27, 1968. There was dancing in the streets. Montreal was still basking in the glory of Expo 67; it was felt that there was nothing the city couldn't accomplish. There was just one problem: Montreal didn't have a stadium. Mayor Jean Drapeau suggested that the Autostade be used as temporary quarters until the city could build a domed stadium, but that idea fell through when a lease couldn't be worked out with the Alouettes who were playing their games there at the time and had a three-year lease.

To make matters worse, some of the ten men who had committed to putting up a million dollars each began dropping off, until finally only Charles Bronfman was left as a financier.

An initial payment of $1.2 million was supposed to have arrived at league headquarters by August 15, but as August 1 rolled around, the money was nowhere to be found and the *Chicago Tribune* announced that "Major League Baseball's first international experiment is going to flop and Montreal's National League expansion franchise will be forfeited." According to the *Tribune*, the franchise would instead be awarded to Buffalo.

This is where I enter the picture.

As luck would have it, a media team from Montreal had challenged a media team from Ottawa to a game of basketball, played on the court of Carleton University. Having played a good deal of basketball for Macdonald College, I was on the Ottawa team and was pleased to meet up with my old friend Dick Bacon who was Sports Director of United Press International when I was there. He had since moved onto the sports desk at the *Montreal Gazette* and was playing basketball for the Montreal media team.

Following the game, Dick and I went out for a couple of beers to talk about the good old days at UPI, and somehow the conversation came around to the dilemma facing the Expos.

"No question," said Dick, "if we can come up with a stadium, Bronfman will come up with the money. Otherwise, a major league team for Montreal is in the dumper."

Without for a moment thinking anything would come of it, I mentioned Jarry Park, where I had played several times as the second baseman for the DuPont of Canada fastball team. "You know," I told Dick, "Jarry Park, up in the northeast end of Montreal, is a huge facility. You could probably seat twenty-five or thirty thousand people there if you removed a couple of the existing softball diamonds. There's tons of parking and it's close to the Trans-Canada Highway."

Dick's response was a kind of grunt, but according to a story in the *Montreal Gazette*, Dick Bacon did mention Jarry Park as possible site to his good friend, sportswriter and broadcaster Russ Taylor. Then, and this is very well documented, a couple of days later, Russ Taylor along with another sports writer, Marcel Desjardins, escorted John McHale, Deputy Commissioner of Major League Baseball, Bowie Kuhn, an attorney for the National League, and Warren Giles, President of the National League, to Jarry Park to have a look. Fortuitously, there was a semi-pro baseball game underway; some of the fans recognized Giles, and stood up shouting "Le Grand Patron."

Impressed, the men looked around, determined that the three thousand seats could in fact be expanded to accommodate thirty thousand,

and right then and there they gave Jarry Park the official seal of approval. Charles Bronfman lived up to his word and put up the necessary money, and the rest is history.

On April 14, 1969, the Montreal Expos hosted the St. Louis Cardinals at Jarry Park in front of 28,456 fans and treated us all to an 8–7 win. Three days later, Bill Stoneman pitched a 7–0 no-hitter against Philadelphia, and the possibilities seemed boundless.

Would the Expos have come to Montreal if I hadn't mentioned Jarry Park? Who knows? But it's possible. But please don't blame me for all the broken hearts the Expos left behind when they abandoned Montreal.

I Help Joe Carter Win the '93 World Series!
(or The Bubbling Bliss of Yogic Flying)

Well, to be totally honest, that headline about helping Joe Carter may be a bit of a stretch. But then again, not according to more than one Toronto baseball fan.

Just in case you've forgotten, or because it was Toronto and you tried to forget, the year is 1993. The Toronto Blue Jays are competing for their second World Series title in a row. The year previous they defeated the Atlanta Braves in a thrilling battle which saw the World's Championship going to a team from outside the United States for the first time in history.

Toronto, indeed much of Canada, is abuzz with excitement. Can the Jays really win two in a row? It certainly appears so. The Jays are leading the Philadelphia Phillies three games to two as the series heads back to Skydome for game six scheduled for October 23.

It's October 22. I've got a three-hour talk show to prepare and I'm looking for a brainwave. The only thing Toronto wants to talk about is the series and, in particular, the big game tomorrow during which the Jays can once again win it all. That's fine and dandy, but three hours of callers, many of whom would have difficulty telling the difference between a baseball glove and an oven mitt, predicting a big Toronto win can get pretty boring. It's not a sports show I'm running. I can't get into batting averages, and since everyone pretty well agrees that the Phillies' John Kruk is about the most unathletic-looking bird they have ever seen, where's the controversy? Where's the fun?

And then it hits me. What we need here is a good old-fashioned levitation of Skydome.

The yogic flying craze is at its peak in the early 1990s. Yogic flyers from around the world are bouncing for peace in various world capitals. The Natural Law Party, featuring yogic flyers clad in white trousers and T-shirts decorated with the party's rainbow symbol, was founded in Britain by Maharishi Mahesh Yogi only two years previously and claims to have branches and millions of adherents in more than sixty countries. John Hagelin has just announced that he is the Natural Law Party candidate for the US Presidential election in 1995.

Maharishi Yogi is telling us that "yogic flying cultures the ability to think and act in a settled level of awareness and gain mastery of natural law." He describes the experience during yogic flying as one of "bubbling bliss!" I'm not making this up. I couldn't! "The mind-body coordination displayed by yogic flying shows that consciousness and its expression—the physiology—are in perfect balance. Scientific research has found that maximum coherence in brain functioning gives rise to yogic flying." Really, that's what the Maharishi is saying, and some people are taking him seriously.

"So, what the heck," I'm saying to myself, "if levitating the body is such a bubbling, blissful thing to do, just imagine the benefits of getting Skydome to do a bit of flying, yogic or otherwise!"

What's needed in order to set the stage properly and get mind and body coordinated is a good solid bout of chanting. Almost any mantra will do, they say, but the only one I'm familiar with is where you get a kind of hum going in the back of your throat and maybe a bit up into your nose until it sounds something like AAHHHHUM-MMMM; AAHHHHHUMMMMM; AAHHHUMMMMMM. You probably do it all the time when you want to get your brain in sync with your body!

So I do the only thing any talk-show host worth their salt would do under the circumstances, I ask my listeners if they'd like to take part in a life-altering experience and help to levitate Skydome and thus get the Blue Jays into a proper bubbling bliss frame of mind so they can pound the grubby, long-haired, unshaven bums from Philly into dog dirt.

"I'm taking on-air chanting and mantra auditions right now," I tell my audience. "I've nine phone lines coming in here, I will take the nine best AAHHHHHHHUMMMMMMMs, and together we'll all AAHHHHHUMMMMMM at the same time until we get Skydome doing a big of levitating. Those of you who can't get through on the phones, I'm going to give a countdown, so when I say three—two—one—I want everyone—the nine on the phone—and the thousands of you out there in your homes, your cars, your offices…wherever you are to AAHHHHHUMMMMMM all together until we get that Skydome up and, if not flying, at least bouncing."

The phone lines immediately light up like "shock and awe" day in

Iraq! I make each of the nine phone callers give me a little audition, and then, after we've got them all in a row, a couple of practice runs, and finally, the real thing.

The excitement mounts. Curious, puzzled and giggling office staffers at CFRB begin to filter into the control room in front of me. I wave them into the studio with me. What the heck, the more the merrier, or better flying or whatever!

So now we've got about 20 people in the studio—nine callers on the phone lines and heaven only knows how many thousands of people out there in radio land all ready to launch. I extend the drama a bit more and insist that my studio audience, which now includes two of the barbers from the shop below, do a bit of rehearsing. Finally, we're ready!

"Okay," I say, "everyone ready? Don't forget, on my count of three, two, one…" There are nods in the studio and a chorus of ascent on the phone.

"All right then, and please, those of you anywhere near Skydome, please as quickly as possible report back to me here with your observations. If you have a tape measure, check to see how much the stadium levitated, and if you have a stopwatch, let us know how long it stayed in the air. We're going to do this very scientifically."

"All right now—all together—on the count of—THREE—TWO—ONE: AAAAAHHHHHHHHUMMMMMMMMMM; AAAAAHHHHHHHUMMMMMMMM; AAAAHHHHHHUMM-MMMMMMMM." There's loud laughter. "No laughing, no laughing," I yell. "Again, let's hear it with a bit more feeling this time. I want to hear it coming up from Yonge Street; come on you cabbies, we need you to lead this thing out there on the streets. Okay—one more time—all together now—THREE—TWO—ONE: AAAAAHHH-HHHHHUMMMMMMMMMM; AAAAAHHHHHHHUMM-MMMMM; AAAAHHHHHHUMMMMMMMMMM."

This time the old CFRB building is almost shaken off its foundations at Yonge and St. Clair. When we all stop laughing, I thank all nine callers, congratulate them on a marvelous job and ask for reports from Skydome. The first few callers are killing themselves laughing. All admit they took part in the chanting when they weren't busy rolling on the floor with laughter.

Then comes "the call!"

It is a young man, slightly breathless, very excited. I still have the recording and relate it here word for word.

"Was it you who just did that chant thing?" he asked. I confessed. "My God," he gasps, "I was driving past the Skydome when I heard this funny sound coming out of my radio. For some reason I happened to just glance over to the stadium—to Skydome—and I swear the whole place seemed to lift up a couple of inches and tilt over to the left!"

I decide to play it as straight as he's giving it to me. "Thank you very much, Gerry is it? Yes, Gerry. You didn't happen to have a chance to measure how much the stadium levitated did you?" There is a brief pause. "Not really, actually I don't know about levitating, it just seemed to kind of tilt, just for a moment or two to the left—like towards left field, I'd say."

I keep him on the line for a couple more minutes, trying to coax something even more outrageous out of him, but he just keeps repeating about Skydome tilting over to the left.

As you can imagine, subsequent callers think the call is hilarious, and then a young female caller says something, which the following day sends shivers up my spine.

"Well," she says, "now that Skydome has been tilted towards left field, that should make it easier for the Blue Jays to hit some home runs there!"

Fast-forward to the next day, October 23, 1993. Leading the series three games to two, the Jays look as if they've got it all sewn up as they head into the seventh inning with a five to one lead. Veteran pitcher Dave Stewart is on the mound for the Jays, and many of the fans know that only two teams in World Series history have ever come back from being four runs down in the seventh inning while facing elimination. The mood in the stands is one of joyous celebration. A second World Championship is only a few minutes away.

The mood quickly sours when that freaky little Philly pest Lenny Dykstra belts a home run with two men on, and suddenly the Jays' lead has been cut to five to four. The Jays call in relief pitcher Danny Cox, but, oh my gosh, he gives up two singles, there's a stolen base, then a double, and by the time the inning is over, the scruffy Phillies are leading six to five. You can hear a pin drop in the stands.

There are no runs in the eighth inning. Then, in the ninth, Philly manager Jim Fregosi calls in their leading closing pitcher, Mitch Williams, otherwise know as "The Wild Thing."

Williams walks Ricky Henderson. Devon White flies out to left field, then Paul Molitor raps out his third hit of the game. The stands come alive again! Up to the plate strides Joe Carter. Ball one. Screaming in the stands begins in earnest. Ball two. The place goes wild. Williams fires in his third pitch for a strike. The sound drops several decibels. Carter fouls off the next pitch. The count is now even two and two, and the crowd is on its feet. Williams' best pitch is the low fast ball. He places it perfectly. Carter swings and...you know the rest. Over—yes, that's right—over the left-field wall and the Jays win! Who can forget Carter's joyous leaping run from third to home plate? It's one of the great moments in Canadian sports history.

Did our little yogic flying mantra play a role? Caller after caller on my show the next day swear up and down it was the "tilted" field that won it for the Jays. "Please, please, please do it the next time the Leafs get into the playoffs," begs one young man.

"No," I reply, "not even levitation can save the Leafs!"

The Green House

The rambling, drafty old house Kitty and I have moved into on the Carmen Road near Wakefield, Quebec, is a wonderful place to raise our two daughters. A big outdoor winter rink in the front yard, a ramshackle, semi-falling-apart tree house in a backyard apple tree, and acres and acres of grass upon which to frolic. While there may have been much splendour in that grass, it nonetheless took well over an hour to cut, even with a riding mower. So during my daily morning on-air chat with Ken "The General" Grant, which we call "The Green House," I am extolling the virtues of having my eldest daughter's new boyfriend cut the lawn for me, when all hell breaks loose!

We call the five-minute show "The Green House" because it's broadcast live from a small studio we've set up in a den at the rear of the house in which we, the Greens, live. A kind of radio "Seinfeld," Ken and I trade stories about recent adventures, real or imagined, the joys of raising young families, and the craziness of life in general. It is one of the most popular shows I've ever done.

Who can't relate to my story (real) of our purebred pure-white Samoyed dog Nikki (Wild Dog of the North) getting stuck under our porch after giving birth to a half dozen puppies? The fact I had to attack the porch with an axe to free her only to find that despite having paid an exorbitant fee to have Nikki bred to a champion Samoyed male (also white), all six puppies are a perfect match for our neighbour's black and white mutt had listeners howling with laughter. I myself didn't find it all that funny, but that's another story!

So this morning I'm joyfully watching Danielle's newest boyfriend, Paul Gravel, gracefully swooping back and forth across the broad expanse of our backyard with the riding mower as I explain to Ken and our listeners the delicate intricacies of convincing boyfriends to do your work for you, when I spot something amiss. "Geez Ken," I say with some anxiety, "I think the guy is falling asleep out there on the mower! Holy cats…LOOK OUT!"

But it's too late. In a flash, the mower takes a hard right turn and heads directly for the window through which I am watching in horror. The mower, blades whirling at full throttle, rips into the back porch with a crash and throws up a cloud of dust, smoke, grass and splinters. Thankfully, all of this awakens the young snoozing Mr. Gravel, who unleashes a scream that so penetrates the window and walls of the den that it is clearly heard in the living rooms and kitchens of thousands of homes as far away as Quebec City. All of this, you must understand, is being broadcast live to an incredulous radio audience, several of whom are so concerned they phone police to report some kind of disaster at the Greens' house!

By the time our snoozing friend comes to his senses and turns the mower off, it has plowed a 36-inch wide furrow across several feet of wooden deck, stopping only inches before crashing through the window and into my tiny studio. His face is ashen, horror-stricken! When through the glass he can see me doing a live play-by-play, he becomes so befuddled I am afraid he may start up the mower again and either come charging through the glass at me, or more likely turn it around and head for the nearby Gatineau Hills. My "sign off" is one of the least professional you're likely ever to hear. "Geez Murphy, Ken, I've got to go before this guy either kills himself or me. Bye!" It's all there in our archives.

The boyfriend, Paul Gravel, and I make a deal. A summer of cutting my lawn as payment for the furrowed deck, but with one proviso: He has to have at least eight hours sleep before even approaching the mower.

Today Paul Gravel is a commercial pilot operating out of the tiny Caribbean Island called Mustique. His passengers often include some of the world's leading celebrities. Since I have received no word of plane crashes in that neck of the woods, I can only assume he gets lots of sleep!

• • •

The kite flying episode is one I would sooner forget. Radio technology has progressed a little bit by this time, so we're able to take our microphone outside "The Green House" and, if the spirit so moves me, broadcast our daily morning program strolling around the grounds. Being located less than a mile from Gatineau Park, this can get very interesting upon those occasions when bears clamber up one of our apple trees, or deer take up grazing in the front yard.

It's a wonderful late-spring day with a decent breeze blowing, so I decide a live broadcast of some kite flying might be just the perfect thing for our poor city-bound listeners. I've bought one of those huge box kites, and somehow with the assistance of daughters Lianne and Danielle and half the neighbourhood, we've actually got the thing assembled and ready to soar. Some smart guy has convinced me that the best way to fly these big jobbies is with the aid of a good fishing pole with a spinning reel. "Instead of the string which you've got to unwind by hand," he says, "just hook the kite up to the leader on your fishing line and let her rip!"

And he's right. "It works perfectly," I tell Ken Grant and our listeners. "Would you just look at that thing soaring at the end of my line? Know what? This is more fun than fishing!"

The reel sings as I let out some more line, and then I crank it in just for the fun of it, at which point five-year-old Lianne thinks this looks pretty cool and demands a turn at the controls. "Don't be a hog, Daddy," she says, "give me a try."

The microphone picks up every word. "Yeah," says General Grant from his Isabella Street studio, "don't be so mean; give your daughter a try."

You know what happens. A mighty puff of wind, the fishing rod flies out of her little hands; I let a yell out of me. We give chase but to no avail. Rod and reel and kite go soaring off into the wild blue yonder. I've got to describe this foolishness to our listeners. Lianne is crying; Kitty who's been observing all of this with a jaundiced eye is killing herself laughing, so is The General and I suspect most listeners, but I'm worried.

Where is this thing going to come down? Visions of startled motorists and traffic jams dance through my head. A fishing rod and reel soaring high overhead, or landing in your backyard, is not something the average person sees frequently. Stories of alien invasions have been launched with less provocation. Is Wakefield or maybe Chelsea to become another Roswell, New Mexico? I broadcast a warning to be on the lookout for a flying fishing rod and sign off with trepidation and riotous laughter from The General.

It isn't until the next day that someone points to a small story in *La Droit* newspaper. Seems someone had thrown a fishing pole up into some hydro wires and blacked out a couple of hundred homes in Pte-Gatineau.

No word about a kite.

CFRA put a lot of advertising dollars behind the show. Above is an ad that ran in both Ottawa dailies in November 1967.

At left, an ad that ran in the Fall of 1968.

Roar!

In the 1960s and '70s, and well into the '80s, the annual Press Club Ball, staged by the National Press Club, was the number one social event of the year in Ottawa. Here, Fred Davis of "Front Page Challenge" fame, who launched his career at CFRA, CFRA General Manager Terry Kielty, and News Director Campbell McDonald, broadcast the 11:00 p.m. news on CFRA and our sister station, CFMO. These three got all the glory, but I was the one back at the station writing and editing their stories.

NATIONAL RADIO AND TELEVISION AWARD to CFRA

CFRA Vice President and General Manager Terry Kielty accepting A.C.R.T.F. Trophy from Paul L'Anglais, President, Association Canadienne de la Radio et de la Television de Langue Française.

The A.C.R.T.F. Trophy — awarded to CFRA — "The English station which has made the best editorial efforts during the year 1968, to foster the comprehension and support of the French fact's importance to the achievement of Canadian unity."

The A.C.R.T.F. Trophy was awarded to CFRA as a result of the editorial views expressed by LOWELL GREEN and the "GREEN LINE" program, and for his continuing effort to help foster an understanding of the French fact.

CFRA-580
Ottawa's First News Voice

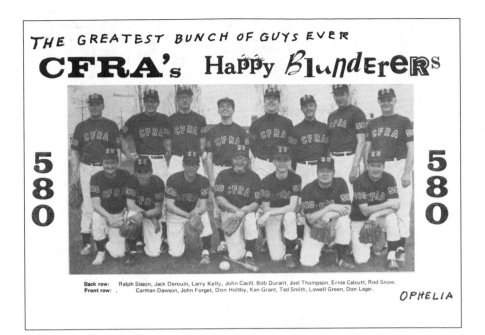

THE GREATEST BUNCH OF GUYS EVER
CFRA's Happy *Blunderers*

580   580

Back row: Ralph Sisson, Jack Derouin, Larry Kelly, John Cavill, Bob Durant, Joel Thompson, Ernie Calcutt, Rod Snow.
Front row: . Carman Dawson, John Forget, Don Holtby, Ken Grant, Ted Smith, Lowell Green, Don Leger.

OPHELIA

One of the most ardent Happy Blunderers fans was someone named named Ophelia. We never met Ophelia, we never talked with Ophelia, but she or he constantly sent us various kinds of cards and mementoes of our games in various Ottawa Valley towns. This picture is classic Ophelia—a picture of the Happy Blunderers in their heyday made up as a Christmas card, which was subsequently sent to each one of us in the photo.

Facing page: In 1968 and '69, as tension between English and French bubbled to a boiling point in Quebec, I launched a series of radio editorials broadcast across Canada calling for calm and understanding. Many of us were afraid that if things didn't calm down, civil war might actually break out. For my efforts, the Canadian Association of Radio and Television Broadcasters presented me with a special award for representing, in their words, "The English-language radio or television station which contributes the most comprehensive broadcasting to foster the comprehension and support of the French fact's importance to the achievement of Canadian unity." Station Manager Terry Kielty accepted the award on behalf of the station. Shortly after that, Prime Minister Pierre Trudeau sent me a letter praising my endeavours and congratulating me on the award.

Yes, that's Max Keeping on the right, shortly after he arrived at CFRA in the mid-1960s. As you can see, Les Lye seems anything but impressed.

Believe it or not, this is guitarist Joe Turner (with the beard) and everyone's favourite Irish tenor, Robin Avril, prior to one of their annual Christmas Cheer performances, *circa* 1972.

A somewhat younger Wayne Rostad at the same Christmas Cheer broadcast, taking liberties with our Christmas tree. This year will mark my 40th appearance on this program (or is it the 41st?) which has raised millions over the years for Christmas baskets for those in need.

It's municipal election night 1975. CFRA news anchor Don Leger (left), Gary Guzzo, who went on to become a family court judge, then an MPP, and I tell our listeners that Lorrie Greenberg is about to become the City's first Jewish mayor.

July 1, 1978. The final broadcast of "The Greenline," which at the time was the longest running open-line show with one host in Canada. Among those wishing me well was Prime Minister Pierre Trudeau. For the occasion, Bayshore Shopping Centre dispatched a blond, bikini-clad model to speed me on my way. My father, who shared that last program with me, appeared to be far more interested in the model than he was in Trudeau!

ABOVE: I don the goalie pads for a special promotion between periods of an Ottawa 67's game. On the left is John Caines, who hosts "The Ren Molner Show" on CFRA today, and on the right is none other than CFRA "Experts on Call" host Ray Stone, all decked out in his wife's skates and a strange object over his shorts! If you can identify any of the others, please let me know. It was

during one of these promotions that the late Brian Smith, known everywhere as Smitty, and I feared our careers had been cut short.

LEFT: Ken "The General" Grant, in full uniform, waves to the crowd as I captain the ship along the Rideau Canal during the first Tulip Festival Canal Flotilla in the spring of 1975. Both The General and I played a major role in organizing and promoting the Flotilla, which has since become an integral part of the annual Tulip Festival.

Smitty

It's the summer of 1982. CJOH sportscaster Brian Smith and I are teamed up with a couple of politicians in a charity golf game in Metcalfe. I won't use names here, since both politicians are now in business in our province. What I will say is that while one of our new teammates was a real sweetheart of a guy, the other was a pure, unadulterated jerk of the first order!

Some would have a less complimentary term, but since this is a family book I won't go there. Our friend Mr. Jerk starts getting his jollies during the introductory handshakes when he refers to Brian and me as disc jockeys. Giving his political compatriot a poke in the ribs and what he believes is a conspiratorial wink, he says, "Well, I guess we'll just have to give our disc jockey friends here a lesson in the game of golf." Brian, or Smitty as we all called him, and I just look at each other. We've been through this kind of stuff before. For sure, it was going to be a long afternoon!

It soon becomes evident that Mr. Jerk considers himself a very fine golfer and after a couple of holes he begins providing both Brian and me with little helpful hints about stance, swing and grip. All interspersed with anecdotes about famous people he has played with in the past and how much they were in awe of his abilities. He also makes it abundantly clear that basic rules of the game really don't apply to him. We have to pretend we don't see him nudge a ball with his foot out of the rough on the 4th hole. On the 5th he jams one behind a tree and takes an eight, but claims his handicap is such that it won't allow him to take anything more than a bogey five. And so it goes. I've played a few games with some real horse patooties in the past, but this guy takes the cake. I try impressing him with a story of my game with George Knudsen during the Canadian Open, but he's not the least impressed; in fact, he manages to one-up me with a story about Al Baldwin suggesting he should abandon politics and turn "pro." At that I just grit my teeth and shut up.

Now I want you to understand that while in those days I was a fair golfer, usually able to shoot in the low 90s, Brian Smith was close to a scratch golfer. He may even have been one at that time. For those of you who don't play golf, that means he was one heck of a great golfer, as are many former NHL players.

So I am a little puzzled, as it becomes evident that Smitty is not having a very good game this day. Approach shots just miss the green. Three-foot putts he should drain just stray a tad to the right or left. Mr. Jerk is having a ball, beating Smitty on almost every hole and chortling with glee. By the time we make the turn at the 9th hole and head for the 10th, Mr. Jerk is completely ignoring his fellow politician and me and has now begun referring to Smitty as "the puck chaser." At one point when Smitty misses a very short putt, Mr. Jerk says something about "maybe that's what happens when you play too many games without a helmet." Accompanied always with a loud chortle in appreciation of his own finely honed sense of humour!

I am beginning to wonder if there is a paramedic I can summon from the clubhouse when Smitty finally loses his cool, but what happens next is a thing of beauty.

"Say listen," says Smitty as he prepares to tee off on the tenth, "let's make this a bit more interesting." He turns towards Mr. Jerk. "Our games look to be pretty even here, so what say you and I go head-to-head for a buck a hole, these other guys can do what they want." Mr. Jerk is somewhat offended by the suggestion that Smitty's abilities approach those he possesses, so he's quick to take up the bet. A snort of derision and a suggestion that maybe if Smitty really thinks he's that good, maybe a couple bucks a hole might be more appropriate. Smitty shakes off the two-dollar suggestion. "Naw," he says, "a buck is probably enough, maybe a bit more later." Sensing something is up, we "other two" decline to wager anything on the grounds of lack of skill.

If Smitty was playing poorly on the front nine, now on the back nine he is terrible.

Shots spray every which way, but somehow he always seems to manage to just barely avoid disaster. He scrambles all over the course to even win a hole and tie a couple more.

Now we're at the 14th, with Smitty down six strokes. His betting partner is strutting like a bandy rooster. Crowing like one too!

Smitty lines up his drive—steps back to take a couple of practice swings that look awful. Another swing and he almost falls over. Just as he's about to step into his drive he stops, shakes his head, backs off a step or two and says, "I think I know what's wrong with my game. I usually play for a lot more money than a buck a hole. I think you're probably right, there just doesn't seem to be enough of a challenge here." He comes down off the tee, reaches into his golf bag and pulls out a wad of bills. "What the heck," he says, "the Lord hates a coward; a hundred bucks says I can still win this game." Mr. Jerk rises to the bait like a trout to a fly. "You're on. This is going to be the easiest hundred dollars I ever earned!"

Well, I don't have to tell you what happened.

Not wanting to tip his hand too obviously Smitty manages to beat him by only one stroke. Mr. Jerk, perhaps suspecting he's just been sandbagged royally, takes off in a huff, refusing even to accept the free beer offered.

I wasn't really paying attention, but several months later Smitty calls me with the news that his golfing "partner" has just lost the election.

"I feel kind of bad," says Smitty. "Maybe if he'd had an extra hundred dollars he might have won!" He laughs and hangs up.

It's some time later when Smitty gets me into what I fear may be a career-ending pack of trouble. For the past couple of years I had been part of some between-period entertainment at Ottawa 67's hockey games. Billed as the "mystery goaltender," I don the pads and, having been a pretty fair goaltender in younger days, take on various members of the media in shootouts. The first year I did this I stopped the entire media contingent twice, except for one player. On his second attempt Smitty managed to deke me out and pop one into the net, but the fact that I had stopped a former NHL player was something I didn't mind boasting about to my daughters.

The second year Smitty warned me in the dressing room that there was no way I would stop him this time. "Oh, yeah? Look at this!" I boast. Someone had made me a huge metal shield. A good four feet tall, three feet wide with a small slit to peek through at incoming pucks and a welded-on handle. It had to weigh 25 pounds.

I thought I might just skate around the rink a couple of times with it for a laugh or two, but Smitty has other ideas. "Listen," he says to me, "go into the net with the shield during the warm-up. I'm going to wind up at centre ice and fire a bullet at your head. It should scare the heck out of a few people, but bring the shield up just in time; the crowd will love the bang." I'm a little dubious. "Yeah sure, Smitty, I raise the thing up to protect my head and you shoot my legs out!" "No, no," says Smitty, "trust me!" Foolishly, I do just that.

It works, exactly as planned. Smitty clears everyone on the ice out of the way and starts his windup behind the opposite net. Just across the centre red line he fires a howitzer directly at my head. As per instructions and out of self-preservation, I snap the shield up just in time. CLANGGGGG! My ears are still ringing when I hear the cry for help. The puck has careened off my shield and clocks a guy square in the head up in the fourth or fifth row!

We both rush over to the boards and are assured the injury isn't serious, but the next day Smitty is on the phone to me. "We could be in big trouble," he says. "The guy we whacked had his lawyer call me this morning and asked us both if we could meet them this afternoon at his house. I got the idea we might be able to talk them out of a law-suit." "What do you mean *we* whacked?" I ask. "You whacked him. For me it was just self-preservation."

Smitty pooh poohs my attempt at an alibi, so that afternoon we pull up to a modest bungalow in Barrhaven, ring the doorbell and are confronted with several stone-faced people hovering solicitously around this poor guy sitting on a kitchen chair with a huge blood-stained bandage swaddling his head. We both figure we've pretty well had the biscuit!

We step forward, offer our apologies and shake the victim's hand. He looks like he's on his last legs from a concussion, loss of blood, fractured skull, nerve damage or heaven only knows what. "So wrecked by it," says the guy who identifies himself as his lawyer, "that he probably won't ever be able to work again!"

By this time, I'm figuring maybe I'd better check with my lawyer and my travel agent to book the first flight out of town when suddenly our wounded hero with the bandage starts to giggle. The rest of them in the room can't contain themselves any longer and the room explodes with laughter.

This time it's Smitty and Green who've been had...but good!

If I had been able to track down the photograph they took that day, you would see a little guy with a huge mop-like, red-stained bandage cov-ering a big chunk of his head, standing in front of a kitchen sink with his arms around the shoulders of two slightly sheepish guys sporting very relieved smiles. If you looked closely enough you would see the signatures of Brian Smith and Lowell Green scrawled across the bandage.

Someone once told me he'd attended a party at our victim's house years later and, lo and behold, there hanging in a place of honour on the rec room wall was a beautifully framed bandage with our autographs still clearly visible!

• • •

On August 1, 1995, a mentally ill man shot Smitty outside the CJOH studios in Ottawa. He died the next day.

He was only 54.

It was a terribly sad time for us all in Ottawa. Smitty was one of the most popular figures in the city, always ready to help anyone who needed it. In fact, he was on his way to the Children's Wish Foundation Annual Banquet, which he was going to emcee along with 67's coach Brian Kilrea, when Jeffrey Arenburg pulled the fateful trigger.

But it's the good times with Smitty that I remember best, and to be honest it is those wonderful memories that sometimes make me smile a little bit when I see his sweater hanging from the rafters of Scotiabank Place. I just wish he could be here when we finally win the Stanley Cup!

The Stopwatch Gangster

Canada's most notorious bank robber thought I was his friend. He's even quoted in a couple of newspaper stories and a book he wrote, claiming that I helped him escape from the police. It's all very embarrassing!

I certainly knew Paddy Mitchell. In fact, I knew him from his non-notorious days, when he was just getting started in a life of crime that would place him squarely on both Canada's and the United States' "MOST WANTED" lists.

If you lived in Ottawa in the 1960s and '70s and got out at all, you would be hard pressed not to run into Paddy Mitchell someplace. When they invented the phrase "man about town," they had Paddy Mitchell in mind. He held court most afternoons, and planned robberies, from what we now know, at his favourite table at Sammy Koffman's famous (or infamous) Belle Claire Hotel. I'd run into him several times there. We had a nodding acquaintance. He knew I was some kind of radio guy. I knew he was reputed to be into some kind of crime, but then, at the Belle Claire, who wasn't? (Not me, of course!)

More frequently, I would see Paddy at the Men's Health Club at the YMCA on McLeod Street, where I used to hang out most afternoons playing handball in the 1970s.

Where I didn't see him was on a small bridge leading from the waterfront restaurant of the Delta Vancouver Airport Hotel to the hotel proper in May of 1980. He saw me and it scared the heck out of him, because at the time he was on the lam from police in both the United States and Canada after escaping from prisons in both of those countries.

By this time, Paddy Mitchell, as leader of the Stopwatch Gang, had stolen, by his own estimation, several million dollars in gold bullion from the Ottawa International Airport and from banks from one end of the continent to the other. I won't go into all the details of his exploits, they have been well documented elsewhere, other than to say that because I didn't blow the whistle on him and tell police he was hanging out at the Delta Vancouver Airport Hotel, he was convinced until he died that I was his friend. I didn't mind that so much, but the fact he boasted about our friendship to everyone he knew, including newspaper reporters, was a tad difficult to explain at times. Especially when some of my police buddies came calling with raised eyebrows! Fact is, I didn't see him on that bridge in BC, or if I did, it didn't register on me who he was. Figuring that since he was locked up for the rest of his life in Leavenworth Prison, he needed every friend he could find, and I never told him the truth.

The fact that our paths should cross on that day in May is one of those strange circumstances that sometimes makes you wonder if there's a poltergeist someplace playing tricks on us poor humans.

Neither one of us had ever been in Vancouver before. Paddy Mitchell was hiding out from the law, I was there signing a deal to host an open-line show at CKOY (now Oldies 1310) in Ottawa.

I thought I had retired from the talk show business on July 1, 1978. We had the final "retirement" show on CFRA with all sorts of special guests, including Prime Minister Pierre Trudeau, my father, and a bikini-clad model. (My father was far more interested in the model than he was in the Prime Minister!) A recording of the show went into the National Archives while I set off with three partners, including the co-owner of the Ottawa 67's, Earl Montagano, to launch a new travel agency we called Ottawa Travel.

Things progressed fairly well until we borrowed a huge chunk of money to buy our major competitor, Algonquin Travel. Wouldn't you know it, about the time our first payment on the loan was due, interest rates shot up to about 20 percent and our friendly banker suddenly developed a serious case of the grumps and insisted that our monthly payments more or less be doubled. As if in concert with the banks, my marriage of 19 years fell apart, the bankroll I'd been able to stash away under the mattress was suddenly chopped in half and life stopped being a whole lot of fun.

In the midst of all this delightful entertainment, out of the blue one day I received a phone call from Paul Mattel, General Manager of CKOY. "What would it take to get you out of retirement?" he asked. Never thinking he'd come anywhere close, I blurted out "a hundred thousand." I'll never forget his reply. "Well, I'm not falling off my chair!" He paused for moment, thinking. "My wife and I are leaving tomorrow for a holiday in Hawaii. We'll be at the Airport Delta Hotel in Vancouver tomorrow night, why don't you meet us there in the marina restaurant, let's say at seven for dinner? I'll have a contract for you to sign and we'll be in business." I didn't say it, but I was sure thinking, hey, no problem, a six-hour flight is nothing. For a hundred thousand dollars a year, I'll fly to the moon if you want. This was 1980, don't forget. Today $100,000 is a lot of money; back then, it was a small fortune!

Thus it was that while crossing that little bridge from the hotel to the restaurant to sign a contract for the most money I had ever made in my life, Paddy Mitchell, who used to steal that much before breakfast, thought he'd discovered a new friend!

Too Intelligent

I may be the only person ever fired for being "too intelligent." Well I wasn't actually fired. CKOY chose not to renew my contract, which is the same thing as being fired, since the paycheques dry up.

It's not every day a guy is told he isn't wanted anymore, so as you can imagine, it's something that has stuck in my mind. Stuck in my craw, too, if the truth be known! It's early June 1982, my two-year contract is up for renewal at CKOY, so when Program Director Scott Cameron calls me into his office, I just assume we're about to begin negotiations for another two or maybe even three years.

Before signing my original contract, I had warned CKOY that building an audience, even for someone as well known as I was, would take time and a good deal of promotion. "When a host changes radio stations, as I have done," I told them, "it can take years before even half the former listeners are aware of it, unless there is very strong promotion." Management at CKOY claimed to understand this, but I really think they believed that when I came across to their station, success would be instant with very little effort or expenditure on their behalf. Let's just say the station didn't break the bank promoting the new show.

Despite this, as I came to the end of the contracted two years, my show was starting to build a solid audience. Advertising sales weren't as strong as they had predicted, but J. J. Clarke (now CJOH weatherman) from 6:00 until 8:30 a.m., followed by Lowell Green after the 8:30 news until 11:00 a.m., were starting to eat into CFRA's audience, and the prospects were looking good.

My negotiating strategy was to ask for a $10,000 a year raise in the first two years of a new contract, $15,000 in the third year. If pressed I would drop that by $5,000 a year.

Little did I know!

It was the usual procedure in situations such as these, starting with "Come in, Lowell, close the door, have a seat." Straightforward, standard stuff. And then the two-by-four to the head! "Lowell, you're doing a hell of a job, but we've decided on a change of course here at CKOY, and frankly, Lowell, you are just too intelligent!"

Honest to God, that's what Scott says. "You're just too intelligent."

Unfortunately, whatever intelligence I may have isn't nearly sufficient to figure this one out. "You mean you want me to dumb it down? Is that what're you're saying? You want me to start doing the movie star crap?"

How dumb can you be? Right?

He looks at me rather strangely. "No, that's not it. We're not going to renew your contract.

To this day it just amazes me. As a matter of fact, it amazes me even more today as I understand more about radio than I did back in 1982. Here was a radio station trying to build an audience in the face of very stiff competition. They've got one of the best broadcasters in the country in the fold, but they're going to let him go because he's too intelligent! It wasn't long until J. J. was gone, as well.

Fact is, of course, CKOY never again was able to match the ratings J. J. and I provided, and never again became the force in the market-place that we were creating. There is no question in my mind that had CKOY retained J. J. and me, it could very well be the powerful, profitable community leader that CFRA has become.

Actually, I should have seen it coming, because several months earlier J. J. and I were "treated" to an afternoon with CKOY's radio "consultant." In those days, you've got to understand, consultants were like gods. All knowing, all seeing, all bullshit, as far as I am concerned.

Radio consultants probably destroyed more radio stations and set the industry back further than anything did since the days of Amos and Andy. Radio consultants were living proof of what my father used to say about B.S. baffling brains every time. They had the jargon down pat, claimed to have all the latest hot info from American markets, winning theories sprang out their collective backsides! Talk for ten minutes to one of those guys and your head would spin faster than anything since *The Exorcist*.

I forget this particular consultant's name, but I surely do remember

This is a special promotional piece radio station CKOY sent to advertisers in an effort to get them to buy time on my show. This was prior to having been fired for being "too intelligent!" Having just ended a 19-year marriage, it was an altogether unhappy time for me.

his weirdness. I'm not sure whose idea it was, all I remember is that one day J. J. and I are told we're being rewarded for an especially good ratings book with a trip to an Expos baseball game in Montreal, hosted by our consultant.

We were pretty impressed. This guy was highly regarded by station management. "One of the best consultants in the business," was the word we got.

His office was on Sherbrooke Street, which was, in itself, pretty impressive in those days, until we got there and found that his office consisted of a tiny cubbyhole up three flights of narrow, wooden stairs over some kind of rooming house. Just to add to the ambience, the stairs and his office were filled to overflowing with boxes and boxes of some kind of contest ballot. We never did figure that one out.

J. J. and I were anxious to get out to the Olympic Stadium and soak up a bit of the atmosphere, maybe watch some of the warm-ups. No such luck. This guy says first we have to drop around to nearby Churchill's Pub where he's going to meet Ted Blackman, who was the big name sportswriter and broadcaster of the day in Montreal. So off to Churchill's we go. Our consultant friend takes a seat at the bar, instructing J. J. and me to take a table. What the heck, eh? This is a big-time radio consultant about to meet a big-time Montreal writer and broadcaster. Who are we two bozos from a tiny outpost up the Ottawa River to ask questions?

What happens next tops the charts for weird. Ted Blackman saunters in, greets several fans, waves hello here and there, nods right and left, and then takes his customary stool at the bar. He walks right past our consultant friend without so much as a nod of recognition. J. J. and I are fascinated. Blackman orders a Molson Export. Our consultant orders a Molson Export. Blackman lights up a cigarette. Our consultant lights up a cigarette. I don't recall if they were the same brand, although that wouldn't surprise me. This goes on for a good half-hour or more. J. J. and I are intrigued by it all but would like to get off to the ball game. Finally, Blackman gets up and walks out with some woman. Our consultant gets up. He doesn't walk out with a woman but suggests we head out for the ball game.

At the very least, we were sure what with a big-time radio consultant and all, especially one with an office on Sherbrooke Street, we'd have wonderful seats at the stadium. If not behind home plate, at least along the first baseline.

Are you kidding?! Nosebleed city was more like it. So high up they were handing out oxygen tanks! Well, I'm kidding about the tanks, but if you've ever been treated to the upper echelons of the "Big Owe," you know how small those players looked way, way down there on the field!

But it was on the drive back downtown after the game that this little peach of a person tipped us off to what was in the wind. Ted Teaven was the big name in Montreal radio at the time. He conducted a combination sports-news talk, very high-energy program on my old alma mater, CFCF radio. To give you a clue about what kind of show we're talking about here, if Ted didn't like what you were saying (which was most of the time), he'd give you about 20 seconds of air time, and then open up with a machine gun! Great stuff! He was the talk of the town and had the high ratings to prove it

As we're fighting Montreal traffic during the drive back down-town after the game, we're listening to Ted go through his act. He's so outrageous and funny that J. J. and I start laughing. We think he's tremendous. But what the heck do we know?

In fact, according to our host, Ted Teaven is terrible. "That guy's history," says our consultant friend, pointing to his car radio. "I've already recommended he be fired as soon as his contract is over."

J. J. and I are stunned. "Fired! Why the hell would you want to fire Ted Teaven? He's the best thing CFCF has," is my contention. The consultant looks sideways at me for a moment and confirms what he has suspected all along: I know absolutely nothing about broadcasting.

"Talk shows are the death of radio," he says, "the worst thing that ever happened to the industry. Most people hate them and won't listen to a station that features one, especially a guy like Teaven."

By this time I'm convinced our host is crazy and no one could possibly take him seriously, so it never dawns on me that my days at a talk-show host on CKOY are numbered. "Why is a guy like Teaven so bad for radio?" asks J. J.

Our consultant friend almost snarls, and as best I can recall it says something very close to the following: "Because men are jealous of guys like Teaven. Their testosterone doesn't match Teaven's testosterone and they hate him!" He goes on. "It's the same reason women don't like to hear female vocalists. It makes them crazy jealous. No radio station is ever going to be successful playing female singers to housewives or having guys like Teaven do talk shows."

I know it's hard to believe, but that's pretty well what he said. Mind you, I'd heard the same claims about women not liking female vocalists in my early days in radio, but I couldn't believe the idea was still floating around. As for men being too jealous of male talk-show hosts to listen to their shows, well, the record speaks for itself.

Nonetheless, a few weeks later, I get hauled into an office at CKOY and am told I'm too intelligent to stay on the air. I can't believe it, but it's obviously at the urging of a little bonehead in Montreal, so dumb that he's obsessed with Ted Blackman but can't muster the courage to even say hello!

Ted Blackman died in 2002. If there's any justice in the world, since then our little consultant friend has finally been able to meet him. Thank God, radio "consulting" is more or less a dead industry today!

Bushwhacked by the Somalian Affair!

On March 16, 1993, Somali teenager Shidane Arone is caught attempting to steal supplies from the Canadian Airborne Regiment base in the heart of Somalia. Two members of the Airborne, Corporal Clayton Matchee and Private Kyle Brown, catch Arone and torture him for several hours. Arone dies the next day. Both Matchee and Brown are charged with murder. Matchee later attempts suicide but fails. The attempt causes massive brain damage, making him unfit to stand trial. Brown is found guilty of manslaughter and receives a five-year jail sentence.

Evidence at the trial raises many very disturbing questions. There is testimony that at least sixteen members of the Airborne, including at least one officer, visited the site where and when Arone was being tortured, but they did nothing to stop it. The commander of 2 Commando and a number of his subordinate supervisors are court-martialled and found guilty. The Commanding Officer of the Airborne, Lieutenant Colonel Mathieu, is tried twice by courts martial but acquitted of wrongdoing both times.

Private Kyle Brown always maintains he was a scapegoat and claims he informed every officer he could find of what was happening with Arone and tried to get the torture stopped. He even took pictures of the torture, he said, to provide evidence. When those pictures are published on the front pages of almost every newspaper in Canada, the public becomes outraged and the newly elected Liberal Government under Jean Chrétien orders a full-scale inquiry, which becomes known as the Somalia Inquiry under Federal Court Judge Gilles Létourneau. As more and more damaging information concerning the Airborne comes to light in 1995, Minister of National Defence David Collenette orders that the regiment, which has had a very proud history, be disbanded.

The mess isn't over. The Chief of Defence Staff, General John de Chastelain, who did not support the order to disband the Airborne, resigns. His successor, Air Force General Jean Boyle, is forced to resign only a few months later when he blames his subordinates for previous wrongdoings under his command. Minister of National Defence David Collenette is also forced to resign, at least partially due to the Somalian Affair.

As more and more evidence of military and government cover-ups comes to light, the Chrétien government suddenly announces that the Somalia Inquiry is being cancelled, and on July 2, 1997 the Commission issues a partial report which makes it very clear that the inquiry is being choked off to spare the government further embarrassment.

One of the Commissioners, Peter Desbarats, Dean of Western University's Graduate School of Journalism, is so incensed at the cancellation of the inquiry he writes a book entitled *Somalia Cover-Up: A Commissioner's Journal,* in which he lashes out at the government for taking such unprecedented action and the media for not protesting more loudly. Desbarats writes: "We achieved the dubious distinction of being the first public inquiry in Canadian history to be terminated by a government—for blatantly political reasons—before its work was completed."

Throughout the entire inquiry, and especially when those horrible pictures of Arone were featured on the front page of the *Ottawa Sun,* I was extremely critical of the actions of what I described as a small group of rogue soldiers who had disgraced the Airborne. I, as well as every decent human being, deplored what had happened to the Somali teenager. A few callers to my show tried to defend the torture on the grounds that Arone was caught trying to steal from the regiment, but the record very clearly shows that I shot those people down in no uncertain terms. The station received four complaints that I was too supportive of the Somalis.

When the government abruptly cancelled the Somalia Inquiry and the Commission was forced to release its unfinished report, I was outraged and the next morning July 3, 1997, I went after the government with all barrels blazing.

I have found over the years that one of the best methods of attack is to use sarcasm, or, as the Canadian Broadcast Standards Council later stated, "the tongue-in-cheek approach."

In as facetious a manner and tone as I could muster, I signed on my program that day with the following words:

"I don't understand what all the fuss is about. Headlines everywhere about the Somalia Inquiry Commission. The Commission should have been shut down a long time ago. Look, Art Eggleton is right. The government is right for a change. I mean after all, let's face it, it was only about a couple of Somalis here, for God's sake. Okay? Come on, come on. All this fuss, all this expense, over a couple Somalis!"

I continued, "This country would be a heck of a lot better off if we didn't have a bunch of wimpy newspeople hanging around trying to pry into things that are none of their business, creating problems. And as for the Commission itself, well let's have a look here. No question. Art Eggleton is right.

"The Commission is the real problem. These guys just don't get it. These guys don't understand. The Commission should have left well enough alone, okay? That was the intention, I mean, find a few people at the lower echelons, guilty of excessive zeal, that's what's involved here, and then let the military high command handle it. Come on, I mean we already jailed Kyle Brown. Why do we have to go any further than that? If there's anything wrong here, it's a couple of overzealous soldiers who succumbed to front-line stress. Let's leave it at that. And let's not forget something else. The Canadian public has spoken on this matter. The Somalia Inquiry was cancelled by Doug Young (the Defence Minister). The Canadian people approved of that. The Canadian people re-elected the Liberal Government to another majority government. The entire Somali issue wasn't even a campaign issue at all. The public understands very well. There's been far too much fuss and bother over a couple of Somalis, for God's sake!"

I went on to say things like "God bless Art Eggleton. God bless Jean Chrétien and the Liberal Government. They understand what the public wants. All this fuss over a couple of Somalis, a couple of wogs. Come on give us a break. Let's get on with the real problems in this country. I mean there's a front-page editorial, or at least a leading editorial in the *Ottawa Citizen* today, deploring the fact that Heritage Minister Sheila Copps didn't give the Queen a curtsy yesterday. Others are upset because Preston Manning took his jacket off. No, *those* are the real problems. Perhaps we should have some sort of inquiry into that kind of thing!"

Now I admit, just reading this sounds pretty bad. Saying it as I did, however, with sarcasm and at times actually sneering at the government, and you get an entirely different picture. Especially when you consider that for days I had been pounding the government over the entire Somalian affair and, in particular, I had been highly critical of the Inquiry's cancellation.

I thought throwing in the bit about one of the real problems being the fact that Sheila Copps hadn't curtsied in front of the Queen could leave no doubt in anyone's mind what I was doing and how I really felt.

Let's face it, the method I used to get my point across is very common in the English language. "Nice tie," you might say to someone, and he would immediately know you meant just the opposite. If I write "great weather," you would think I meant just that. But expressed in a certain way during a blizzard, surely no one could mistake the real meaning.

But on July 3, 1997, one person claimed they didn't understand. That person, not anyone from the Somali community, by the way, complained to the Canadian Broadcast Standards Council (CBSC) that my statements constituted hate-mongering against Somalis and compared me to Hitler. Incredibly, despite even the CBSC understanding fully that in fact I was supporting the Somali community and criticizing the government, the Council, in effect, hung me out to dry as a racist.

Standard procedure when the CBSC receives complaints is that they are referred back to the station for response. In this case, CFRA News Director Steve Winogron, who has done this many times, did an excellent job of pointing out what, in fact, I was doing.

The following is part of Steve Winogron's response to the allegations against me, dated July 17, 1997:

Further to your complaint letter regarding "The Lowell Green Show" of July 3, 1997, I have now had the opportunity to review a tape of the program segments in question.

CFRA could not agree with you more. To hold the view that killing anyone because they are of a particular colour or creed is reprehensible. To whitewash a federal inquiry looking into two such deaths, unconscionable.

Lowell Green has a well-established history of speaking up for the underprivileged, the underdog, the discriminated against. Spending countless hours talking about the greatness of Canada, even producing a nationally syndicated feature called "Lowell Green's Canada."

Federal regulations refer to "a reasonably consistent listener over a reasonable period of time" and anyone who has heard even a few episodes of "The Lowell Green Show" knows he has been an adamant critic of the government's cancellation of the Somalia Inquiry. He had thoroughly denounced the government on numerous occasions for "using its power to hide the truth." And for pretending nothing unacceptable ever happened in Somalia.

Hearing the tape of the program and putting it in its proper context, it is abundantly clear that Lowell was being facetious when he made the remarks in question and throughout the remainder of his three-hour program.

Here, Steve quotes directly from some of the introductory statements I made and says:

If anyone still has not understood the criticism being leveled at the government and its response to the Inquiry findings, Mr. Green makes it obvious when he says God bless Art Eggleton and he further criticizes by saying the idea that the military is subject to the same kinds of laws that apply to the rest of the county is absurd. Of course they aren't.

The tone, delivery, style and context in which these statements were made make it abundantly clear that Lowell was being harshly critical—underscoring the value of human life and criticizing the government's whitewash through the use of appropriately cynical commentary.

The one person who complained did not accept this explanation and he demanded the matter go to the Regional Council of the CBSC for adjudication.

Incredibly, the Canadian Broadcast Standards Council ruled against me and my goose was cooked.

The following is the CBSC ruling:

The Canadian Broadcast Standards Council has found that CFRA breached provisions of the Canadian Association of Broadcaster's Code of Ethics in its broadcast of an episode of "The Lowell Green Show" of July 3, 1997. In the Council's view, Lowell Green's apparent attempt to use sarcasm and facetiousness to criticize the actions of the Federal Government in shutting down the Somalia Inquiry resulted in abusively discriminatory comment against persons of Somali nationality, contrary to the human rights provisions of the CAB Code of Ethics. While the Council found no fault with Lowell Green's rhetorical device, the CBSC considered that the host's failure to defuse the racially offensive component of his remarks at any point in his show resulted in a Code violation.

Now what you should understand is that while all of this is going on, I know nothing of it. I think at some point Steve Winogron told me there had been a complaint about the July 3 show, but he was dealing with it—but I can't even be sure of that. If, in fact, I was informed there was a complaint, I never gave it a second thought; after all, we had four complaints from other shows at about that time that I was being too supportive of Somalis! I did not, nor do I to this day, have a right to know who my accuser is. Nor did I have the right to speak in my own defence.

You can imagine my shock when about two years later, with absolutely no warning whatsoever, I picked up my morning *National Post* and found a story across the top of one of its pages claiming that I had been found guilty of hate-mongering and racism for calling Somalis wogs!

That was bad enough, but almost immediately I began receiving reports that some terrible things were being said about me on a Somali-language program on the Carleton University Radio Station, CKCU.

I immediately contacted CKCU and asked them to check with the CBSC for the exact wording of their ruling and demanded that any slanderous statements being made about me on their station cease and desist. I pointed out that since I did not speak Somali, I really didn't know what was being said, but inflaming the situation could, in fact, be dangerous for me. I should also point out at this time that the host of the Somali program on CKCU had applied for a job at CFRA and had met at least once with News Director Steve Winogron.

I was able to obtain a translation of some of the things that continued to be said about me on CKCU. In my view they were shocking…references to poisonous snakes in our midst and worse.

Earl McRae, writing in the *Sun*, came to my defence, as did the *Ottawa Citizen* in an editorial, but life for me and my family became, if not a nightmare, very uncomfortable indeed. The phone rang in the dead of night; our cars were broken into in the driveway; my mailbox and even the mailbox of a neighbour with the last name of Green were smashed. There were several death threats. Things became so worrisome that at one point, with Deborah becoming increasingly nervous for our safety, we listed our home for sale with plans to move to a less isolated area. As the attacks continued, our fear changed to anger and we decided to fight back. We delisted our home and I launched a lawsuit against CKCU and demanded that I at least have a chance to defend myself against the Canadian Broadcast Standards Council and its ruling.

Thus it was that on February 1, 1999, I squared off with Ron Cohen, National Chairman of the Canadian Broadcast Standards Council, on my show.

The following is a partial transcript of that program provided by Bowdens Media Monitoring Ltd.:

Lowell Green: (CFRA) Our guest this hour is Ron Cohen, National Chairman of the Canadian Broadcast Standards Council, which has ruled in favour of one person who claimed that, in July of 1997, I was guilty of, quote, hate-mongering against Somalis. A complainant who, by the way, compared me to Hitler. Now everybody...Mr. Cohen, by the way, welcome. And let's shake hands here.

Ron Cohen: Can I correct something you've said so far, in the first sentence?

Green: Well, the original complainant did accuse me of hate-mongering and the reference to Hitler was there!

Cohen: That may have been the case, but I think the important thing to bear in mind is that we dealt with that in a very careful way. We happened to be lucky, maybe, because some of us are from Ottawa and we, therefore, know you a little bit better than perhaps some other people do. And we know you're not guilty of hate-mongering. And I suggest to you that there are other media who have taken what we said out of context. Maybe you should get after the other media, Lowell.

Green: Well, maybe you should. Maybe the Broadcast Standards Council has a responsibility to clear up some of the terrible confusion...I am being smeared from coast to coast here.

Cohen: In fairness, Lowell, okay, our decision, which is on the public record, it's right there, the words are on the Web from the instant that they came out, makes no point whatsoever about you being a racist in any way. We don't believe it. I think that we made that point perfectly clear. But I think that there are some media which perhaps take a cheap shot and they took advantage of a comment that was made in isolation. They took something out of context.

Green: But Ron, the truth of the matter is that the Broadcast Standards Council has agreed with a complainant who accused me of hate-mongering and compared me to Hitler.

Cohen: No, but we didn't agree with that complainant.

Green: You didn't agree? How can that be? I have been censored. This radio station has been censored, and it all stems from one complainant. Am I correct, in that there was only one complainant?

Cohen: Well, you are correct in that. There was only one complainant, but again I think that we can't get ourselves, you know, too bound up in the numbers thing.

Green: I want to tell you, Ron, we're going to keep this very civil, but I'm going to tell you that we're going to have to change our phone number. We've put our house up for sale. Believe me, this is very personal for me and for my family.

A bit further in the program we discuss a letter written by Mr. Cohen to the Ottawa Citizen *concerning an editorial it ran defending me and suggesting that if people don't like what they hear on radio they can simply turn it off.*

Green: Explain to me, Ron, why it is that in the *Ottawa Citizen* I see a letter from you straightening the *Citizen* out on facts concerning the Canadian Association of Broadcasters. Why have I not seen a letter from the Broadcast Standards Council to any newspaper explaining that you did not describe me as a racist? Your only concern in that letter was the way that the CAB was being portrayed. I didn't see any concern about the way I'm being portrayed. I'm the one whose reputation is being dragged through the mud.

We debate this back and forth for a few minutes, and then I bring up another point of concern.

Green: In dealing with something as sensitive as racism, I don't think that this was handled right at all. There's another point here. All of my listeners, the *Ottawa Sun*, the *Ottawa Citizen*, hundreds of callers and letter writers to you and to me, including some Somalis, Ruben Freidman, head of the League of Human Rights of B'nai Brith, they all understood very well what I was really saying—that I was, in fact, defending Somalis—all of those—except for one person. Only one listener and six or perhaps seven members of the Standards Council didn't get it.

Cohen: No, that's not true that we didn't get it. And you know perfectly well because you read the decision. The decision made it very clear at every point in the decision, right from the beginning, that the Council got it, the Council understood perfectly clearly.

Green: So you did get it? Who didn't get it?

Cohen: We understood that you were trying to be sarcastic, facetious, and ironic. You were using rhetorical tools, okay.

Green: But who didn't get it?

Cohen doesn't explain who didn't get it, we get into a discussion concerning whether I can sue the National Post *over what they said, and then I ask a simple question:*

Green: But exactly what is it that I did wrong, Ron? Was I wrong in defending Somalis? Was I wrong in criticizing the federal government for canceling the inquiry?

Cohen: Well, no. As you know, we made it perfectly clear in the decision that any kind of commentary which was for the purpose of criticizing a government policy is always something that the airwaves, in a sense, should be responsible to be doing. The airwaves should be vigilant about those... (*Inaudible*)

Green: But I have to do it in a certain fashion. I can't use sarcasm?

Cohen: No, you can use sarcasm. Again, I think that you probably stretched this principle to the absolute limit.

Green: When we come back from the break, I'm going to ask you this question—do we have to censor our language in order to meet other people's lack of understanding of the English language? That seems to be the crux of it.

Here we took a commercial break after which we played a brief statement from Ruben Friedman of the League of Human Rights of B'nai Brith. His statement is as follows:

"It was extremely clear that he was not promoting hatred against Somalis. What he was doing was highlighting how the government had been indifferent to the state of Somalis."

Green: Ruben Freidman understands perfectly well what I was saying.

He gets it perfectly. Could it be that the Council made a mistake here?

Cohen: No, no, the Council was unanimous and quite clear.

Green: So everybody's out of step. Everybody's out of step but my little Johnny!

We debate various issues for a few minutes, and then I ask Mr. Cohen that which I still feel is the crux of the matter.

Green: Julian Bond, head of the National Association for the Advancement of Colored People, says, quote, "You hate to think that you have to censor your language to meet other people's lack of understanding." Ron, do we broadcasters have to censor ourselves in order to meet other people's lack of understanding? Is that where we are now in broadcasting?

Cohen: We broadcasters, I believe, have to censor ourselves to meet the code which broadcasters themselves set up. Canada's private broadcasters took a major lead, a major initiative in this country a decade ago.

Green: But does that mean we have to broadcast with the understanding that some people aren't going to understand?

Cohen: I think that what we have to do is to broadcast with some sensitivity and knowledge of that fact, but more important, we have to broadcast in a way which is reflective of the codes, the standards which broadcasters themselves have set up.

Green: Right, so we could get the CRTC off our backs. We all know that at any time, our licences can be pulled with no appeal or anything else. And, by the way, one of the things about this is that I have no appeal on this whatsoever. I was accused by only one person. I understand the station knows his name, but I have no idea who this person is. I was not allowed to confront my accuser. I was not allowed to take part in any of the discussions on this, to have any say in this. I am tried *in absentia*, found guilty *in absentia* and sentenced in the press *in absentia* with no right of appeal. Now don't you think there's something wrong with that, Ron?

Cohen: First of all, that isn't of course the case.

Green: It certainly is.

Cohen: No, the station was informed of everything every step of the way.

Green: The station knew that we were losing this?

Cohen: No, the station doesn't sit in on the decision making any more than the complainant does.

Green: Well, don't you think that just as a matter of justice, I should have the right to meet my accuser—at the very least know who it is.

Cohen: If we did that the process would never work. If we tried to do that with everybody it would never happen.

Green: What kind of a system is that where you don't get a chance to even confront your accuser?

We continued in that vein for a few minutes, and then took a commercial break.

Green: Mr. Cohen, I'm very concerned about the makeup of the Council which decided my fate. First of all, the program I have been criticized for, or condemned or censored for, was very clearly highly critical of the Liberal government. One of the members of this Council is Robert Stanbury, a former cabinet minister in the Liberal Government.

Cohen: The other five aren't...

Green: Well, let's talk about the other five. Two are described as, quote, social activists, interpretation, feminists. Nothing wrong with that. But do you really think that a man with a conservative voice, such as mine, criticizing the government—don't you think there is a possibility of bias when one of the members is a former cabinet minister of the government I am criticizing, at least two others are social activist feminists, one I understand is a member of the NDP? What sort of justice is a man with a conservative voice expected to get from that?

Cohen: Total, I assure you!

At this point we began to take some phone calls, almost all of which were from Somalis who claimed I had slandered them, that I was racist and a hate-monger. When I questioned these people, it turned out that none of them had actually heard the program but instead had obtained their information primarily if not exclusively from the CKCU Somali broadcasts.

Ron Cohen's last words on that program of July 3 1997 were: "I want to thank you for the opportunity to have us here. First of all to clarify the issue on the accusations made to you about racism, which are really inaccurate, wrong, and are not something we have ever said."

Unfortunately, the damage was already done. There was a widespread belief in the community, especially among Somalis, that I was guilty of hate-mongering against them when, in fact, I was defending them. In addition, the *National Post* never retracted what it said about me, so the impression was left across the country that I had actually called Somalis wogs and was a racist.

I launched a lawsuit against CKCU, Carleton University's campus radio station, entirely at my own expense. As part of the process, we were required to have a conciliation session with an adjudicator. I sat there for the better part of half an hour watching and listening in utter amazement as full-grown men, CKCU's lawyers, the host of their Somali program and a representative of Carleton, all pretended they didn't understand exactly what I had done. I just couldn't believe that men of that stature could read what Ron Cohen himself has said and still claim that I was hate-mongering and was a racist. I realized that with the limitless funds available to Carleton University and CKCU (they have tax money and libel insurance), I didn't stand the ghost of a chance. They would simply drag this out until I didn't have a cent left. In disgust, I got up and walked out of the meeting. No doubt, they celebrated a great victory!

This entire episode is a prime example of why few Canadian radio stations and almost no television stations have talk shows or programs of any type which deal with contentious issues. As you can see, all it takes is one complaint from one person to label not only a host, but perhaps the entire station, as racist or worse. That's serious enough, but what is really throwing a chill into free and open discussions of controversial topics in the broadcasting industry is the tremendous cost and aggravation involved in dealing with the complaints. There are days when almost all of CFRA News Director Steve Winogron's time is taken up dealing with disgruntled listeners and attempting to defuse the havoc they can create with the CRTC and the CAB.

Each complaint must be responded to, very often in writing and in great detail. If the complainant isn't satisfied with the initial response, he or she can pretty well drive station management crazy with repeated complaints to the CAB and/or the CRTC, all of which must be responded to. Some of the listeners know this very well and do everything in their power to make life as miserable as possible.

I must point out that it is not unusual to have to deal with opposing complaints about a particular show, issue or host. As happened with the Somalia show, we had several complaints that I was too sympathetic towards the Somalis. They all had to be dealt with at the same time Steve Winogron was trying to defend me from the one listener who claimed I was slandering the Somalis!

Complicating all of this is the increasing number of immigrants who come to Canada with absolutely no understanding of democracy or free speech, but are surrounded by swarms of "advisors" (i.e. lawyers) anxious to sniff the noxious fumes of racism around every corner. The advisors understand all the subtleties of the English language very well. They can identify sarcasm and use it frequently themselves, but for the most part those they are "advising" have at best a rudimentary knowledge of English and are thus easily convinced they are being aggrieved. Almost all Somalis who claimed I was a racist admitted they had not actually listened to my show, but had heard about it from others.

As Ron Cohen pointed out during his appearance on my program, the code which the Broadcast Standards Council ruled I had broken was established by the broadcast industry itself through their lobby group, the Canadian Association of Broadcasters.

The intent of the code, no doubt, is to keep Canadian airwaves much purer than those in the United States. Heaven forbid that anyone like Howard Stern should ever set up shop north of the border!

In actual fact, the code and the tremendous power of the CRTC (it shut down a Quebec City federalist radio station not long ago) has created a broadcast industry that is mostly gutless when it comes to key issues of the day. Gutless, because to take a position of any kind will inevitably launch a slew of complaints which most stations just don't want to be bothered with.

Most cities in Canada have radio talk shows, but for every Lowell Green or Rex Murphy talking about immigration or supporting our troops, there are probably a dozen hosts out there going gaga over

Paris Hilton or Lindsay Lohan. Even controversial hosts with high ratings aren't safe, as Rafe Mair discovered in Vancouver!

Till the day I die, I will never forget that on Referendum Day, October 31, 1995, as Steve Madely and I were broadcasting live from Ste-Catherine Street in Montreal, the once proud voice of Anglophones, Montreal's CJAD Radio, featured guests talking about interior decoration and personal hygiene!

American radio and television is filled with debate, discussion, opinion and public participation. Here in Canada, with few exceptions, it's pretty much dueling jukeboxes, American sitcoms, and discussions of the best place on your body to place a tattoo!

As far as I am concerned, if the Canadian Government, the CRTC and the CAB were really interested in promoting meaningful Canadian content, they'd demand an end to the terrible blandness that has befallen my industry.

Lowell Green and Dave Rutherford aren't the problem with broadcasting in this country; it's the guy talking about wallpaper, while all around him voters are deciding the fate of the nation.

The Ratings Wars

If old Bob Service thought some strange things were being done "'neath the midnight sun," you should see what happens during "the radio ratings"!

Actually you do see and hear what happens during the "ratings wars," only you probably don't realize what's really happening. Let me explain.

There are two vital ratings periods for radio in Canada: spring and fall. Just as a minor illustration of how crazy things get, the spring ratings don't actually occur during spring, but rather for an eight-week period starting the first week in January until the first week in March. The fall ratings do occur in the fall, starting right after Labour Day for eight straight weeks. There are also summer ratings, but quite frankly, no one takes them very seriously.

When you consider how important the ratings are and how much money is at stake, the whole process is really quite primitive. Several thousand daily "diaries" are mailed at random throughout the city by a company called the Bureau of Broadcast Measurement, better known in the industry as BBM.

Hopefully in a city the size of Ottawa, somewhere between 1,200 and 2,000 of these diaries will be filled out and returned to be analyzed by BBM. Radio stations have to pay a hefty fee to belong to BBM, and while they aren't compelled to subscribe to the service, you wouldn't stay in business very long if you had no way of informing potential advertisers how many people were listening to your station.

The daily diaries require people to fill out a log, detailing what station they were listening to during every quarter hour of the day. Other information concerning age, education, income level, mother tongue, number of children, and so on, is also obtained. To be honest with you, I have never seen one of these ballots, but the BBM and station management across the country swear up and down they do actually exist and are actually filled in. If you ever get a BBM ballot and I am still on the air, please claim you were listening to me. One ballot is considered to represent several hundred people!

I suspect it will not be long until the whole business of determining listenership enters the twenty-first century. "People meters" are now being used on an experimental basis in several American cities.

The meters, carried by listeners, are able to determine what program is being listened to at any given moment and relays that information to the station instantly. It is obviously a much easier system for listeners, and early indications are that it is much more accurate.

Millions of dollars—no, make that tens of millions of dollars—are at stake. For example, one rating point (one percent of all residents listening to radio aged 12 plus) for the entire station is worth about a million dollars in revenue for CFRA. What a ratings point is worth for other stations I have no idea, but you can certainly see why the "ratings wars" are so important.

This is why during January and February and again in September and October radio stations are jam-packed with giveaways, contests, special promotions, special features, you name it. Anything to induce more people to listen to their particular station and get those ratings up! Television, of course, does exactly the same thing during their "sweeps," which by the way usually occur at a different time than radio ratings.

One of the sacred rules during the ratings period is that no announcer is supposed to even whisper the word "ratings," or refer in any way to the fact that a near life-or-death exercise is underway out there in the community. Since these diaries are often not filled out for a week or two after the actual ratings period is over, these rules apply for at least two weeks after the diaries are supposed to be filled out and mailed back to BBM.

I got myself and CFRA into a lovely little pickle a couple of years ago when, almost two weeks after the ratings were over, a caller phoned claiming among other things that I was such a rude SOB that no one he knew ever listened to my show. I responded to the effect that he must have some very dumb friends then, because my show had the best ratings in town!

Nothing happened until a few weeks later when BBM released the results of the ratings which proved that I was right; in fact, I did have the best ratings in town, by a long shot!

Well, you would have thought I had just set fire to the Parliament Buildings, 24 Sussex and David Suzuki's van! Screams of protest from several other stations. "Foul," they cried. Some stations went so far as to insist that the ratings be declared null and void. The newspapers, of course sensing a Green scandal, picked up the story and tried to make a big deal of it.

I didn't know whether to laugh or cry at the incredible, mind-numbing hypocrisy. Here's why:

The BBM "ratings" give a breakdown of listenership for each 15-minute block of programming, 24 hours a day, for every age demographic. For years my time block, between 9:00 a.m. and noon on CFRA, has shown that we have far more listeners during that time slot than any other of the some 27 radio stations in Ottawa-Gatineau. In the key age group of people aged 12 and older, my ratings are usually about double my closest competitor. In older age groups, they are sometimes triple or quadruple. It's called audience share. CFRA's overall audience share, for example, is generally between eight and nine in the age 12 and over demographic, Monday through Friday. My most recent ratings show me with 19.9 in that age category, almost double that of my nearest rival.

I'm not telling you this to boast, although I am hardly trying to hide my light under a bushel, but what had me laughing so hard about the complaints from other radio stations is that these ratings are always obtained with absolutely no special promotion. No giveaways, no contests, no prizes (other than Steve Madely's day-old fruit cups), no full-page ads, common with other stations during "ratings," just me and the Green Beanies!

One of the stations that complained about my brief mention of "ratings" had just completed a giant gasoline giveaway that snarled traffic for blocks. Another had offered prizes totalling thousands of dollars. Trips to exotic ports were given away; full-page newspaper ads pumped the call letters of radio stations across the city—all during the ratings period.

I'm offering day-old fruit cups as prizes—these other guys are giving away tens of thousands of dollars, but they want the ratings declared null and void, because more than a week after they are over, I use the dreaded word "ratings." The hypocrisy was blinding.

Fortunately, we had station management with the guts to tell the other stations to stop being so damn silly, and the issue finally went away.

Despite the fact that mine is probably the only radio show in Ottawa not giving away a small fortune to hype ratings, guess what, six months later my ratings were up again. The best revenge is winning!

Hanging Up

"**W**hy are you always hanging up on people?" I'm just wrapping up a two-hour book-signing session at a bookstore in the Pembroke Mall when I get hit with the question that drives me crazy. Especially coming from a guy who won't spend a dime on my book, but obviously feels he's entitled to a free stab at embarrassing Green in front of a few dozen fans.

I've got what I think is the perfect answer for this bird and give him my most beguiling smile. "Actually, sir, I do go into the matter at some length in my latest book. I think they have a few copies left here at the store. I'd be glad to sign one for you and you can read what I have to say about the hanging-up issue." I reach for one of the books, knowing full well what his reaction will be. He jerks back like I'm offering him a choice bit of buffalo droppings. Gives me a wave of disgust and stomps away. Perfect!

The truth is I lied to our little Pembroke wise-guy friend. I haven't even mentioned the hanging-up issue in my previous books, but since this little bit of mythology does crop up from time to time, let me deal with it once and for all.

First, you must understand that nothing is more boring than a whole host of callers who agree with everything you say. I find myself at times screaming to myself: WILL SOMEBODY PLEASE DISAGREE WITH SOMETHING I SAY? Thus it is that those callers who want to argue, not only usually get on the show first, but also get to stay on longer. This is especially true if the caller is reasonably intelligent, or so far out in left field he's hilarious. As a general rule, the hotter the argument, the longer it lasts.

The reason so many people think I hang up on callers who disagree with me is that the fights, the arguments, the debates, whatever you wish to call them, are the most interesting part of the show, and as the old saying goes, time seems to fly when you're having fun!

For the most part, I try to run the show like a Senator's hockey game. Fourth-line callers—maybe 30 seconds; third-line—maybe 40; second-line, if they're lucky, might get close to a minute on air. First-line callers, the ones who really have something to add or want to engage in reasonably intelligent debate, get two or three minutes. The odd caller who's really ticked off at me, who rants and raves, may find himself with a four-minute shift. Seldom will a call ever go past that. Attention spans, sorry, just aren't that great anymore.

The only exception is the caller, almost always young and male, who thinks they're going to win a testosterone battle with me by being a smart aleck, or a wiseacre as my granddad used to say. Sorry, you want to get really rude or crude, try to show me up, and you're darn right—you're history.

Keep in mind there is a handful of people out there who regularly use false names to get on the air with the intent of making me look foolish. One of their favourite ploys is to at first pretend they are very reasonable and agree with what I'm saying. Then they will suddenly pounce, calling me names or worse. We've also got a few bona fide nutcases out there, including a religious fanatic in Montreal who will sometimes phone the show thirty or forty times an hour.

My producers, Ronnie Roberts and Mike Murphy, are very solicitous of me and do their best to screen these idiots out, but to be honest, I don't mind them at all. I try to keep the show as close to real life as possible, and let's face it, there are some unholy jerks, idiots, troublemakers and nutbars in the real world. No sense pretending they aren't there. I just wish some of these bozos would spend as much time finding a job, or working at the one they have, as they do trying to drive me crazy!

As further proof of how much the show needs opposing views is the fact that whenever possible I will start the show with a caller who really wants to chew me out, or at the very least has some thoughtful insights into the topics of the day. The same is true following commercial and news breaks. "Any callers mad at me?" I usually ask after a break. If the answer is yes, "Put 'em on. Let's have a go." Ronnie can also signal me through the computer if someone is really hot under the collar or has something new to add. To the front of the line!

It is true that I play a bit of a game with a few regular callers who have made themselves pests and whose opinions I know in advance.

One of my favourites is some guy who calls himself Josh from Montreal. He's about as far left as you can go in this country without volunteering to wipe Castro's behind, and he never misses a chance to bash George Bush, the Americans, Stephen Harper, the Conservatives, and me (not necessarily in that order). My approach with good old Josh is generally to kid him along a bit, make him say something so outrageous even Jack Layton must be sniggering, and then kiss him off. Or, depending upon my mood, I might say something like, "Josh, my boy, this time I'm going to give you all the time in the world to explain your theories as to why the Americans are going to blow up the planet. I'm going to just sit back and hear you talk now. Then at his first word, I'll hang up and introduce another caller. A dirty trick? Yup, and I plan to use it more!

I often picture a successful talk-show host as a kind of male lion, in charge of a large pride. He's king of the jungle, but every once in a while a challenger comes along to test his will, skill and stamina. So far I'm still king. And believe me, it is a jungle out there!

The Room of Babel

"**M**y God," says one of the visitors to the CFRA newsroom at 87 George Street. "It's the bloody tower of Babel!" I'm thinking to myself, "Know something? You're not that far off!" Mind you, according to the Biblical version, it was all different languages they were yammering away in atop old Babylon's famous tower, but here in the newsroom it's all English, thank heavens. But it surely is one great babel of voices here on George Street.

At the top of any hour, you are likely to hear Norman Jack delivering the news on CFRA at one microphone, while only a couple of shin guards away Dave (Voice) Schreiber is on another mic cranking out a sportscast on the Team 1200. Maybe a step and a half behind him, John Brenner leans into his mic to bring listeners on Bob FM up-to-date on the latest business news, while within arms length of him is someone advising Majic 100 listeners to bundle up against a cold snap aimed at the capital. Off in a corner, but still right in the middle of this jumble of raucous voices, is likely to be Shelley McLean trying to conduct an interview for tomorrow morning's "On Target Ottawa." Then, just to add to the confusion and the terrible racket, there's Linda Kinsella with a phone stuck in one ear and her finger jammed deeply into the other as she tries to get information on the latest traffic accident and remain sane!

Please keep in mind, all of this, all of these people, all of these microphones are in an area smaller than the average living room. Except for Linda, who claims she's slowly going deaf from all the noise, everyone is wearing a large set of earphones, which screen out some of the surrounding noise, but the headsets pose another problem. Since they can't hear themselves talk except through the radio feed on their earphones, they often don't really understand how loud they are speaking. At times in that newsroom, you've essentially got four or five and sometimes six people virtually shouting into their microphones, all at the same time. It's not quite up to the level of Scotiabank Place after an Alfie goal during the playoffs, but it's not that far off at times. I've seen visitors, upon opening the soundproof doors and stepping into the newsroom, actually recoil in shock.

The microphones are designed to screen out all ambient sound, but the decibel level often reaches a point where even technology throws up its hands and listeners can easily hear the yelling in the background. When CHUM first launched this system, the complaints flooded in. Some people, thinking there was something wrong with their radios, took them in for repair, but now most listeners seem to have grown accustomed to the noise. Once again, most of the complaints to CFRA are about me! Back to the good old days…

The CHUM concept, of course, is brilliant, as good an illustration of the superiority of private enterprise as you are ever likely to see. Think of it. Four radio stations crammed into a space about the size of your average bomb shelter, all serviced by one central news and sports department. And, not incidentally, all cross-promoting each other. You just can't get much more efficient than that.

The main advantage, however, is that all four radio stations have access to a news and sports department much larger and more experienced than any single station could possibly afford. Most music stations I've ever been involved with would consider themselves very fortunate if they had four or five people in the combined news and sports departments. The CFRA news and Team 1200 sports departments, together, have a contingent of close to 20 full-time and a dozen or more part-time reporters and editors, along with a number of talk-show hosts who have extensive journalism experience. If, as happened this past spring, Mayor Larry O'Brien informs Steve Madely on the morning show that he's so angry at a headline that he's suing the *Ottawa Citizen*, all four CHUM stations have immediate access to the story and the interview. The advantages are obvious.

Believe me, I have many worries about the growing concentration of media outlets by fewer and fewer owners. It is especially dangerous when the ownership of broadcasting stations and newspapers are in the same hands, since it provides government with the means to apply editorial pressure to the print media as well as to broadcasting. (The newspaper now becomes vulnerable to a form of velvet-glove blackmail, understanding that they may stand a better chance of getting approval for the purchase of a TV station, or whatever, if their newspaper takes a more friendly tone towards government policy.)

But in the case of those four radio stations jammed into that little cubbyhole on George Street, there is absolutely no question that the ability to own more than one station has provided significant benefits to listeners and advertisers.

It sure hasn't harmed the profit margins of CHUM either, and provided the new owners don't screw things up royally, their shareholders should be dancing in the streets!

Lowell Green Half-Assed Day

I've received a few honours and awards in my day, but none as strange as that presented on air, April 20, 2006, by the Mayor of Ottawa, Bob Chiarelli. I've got things perking along to a slow boil on a pretty hot topic when the double doors to my studio fly open and in strides the Mayor lugging something under his arm. More than a little taken aback, I try to keep talking in a more or less normal fashion as His Honour settles himself into a chair and pulls a microphone over to his face. At this point I decide it might be a good idea to introduce my uninvited guest, at which point the mayor whips out a framed, inscribed plaque and begins to read the following:

WHEREAS, Lowell Green is celebrating his 50th anniversary in broadcasting; and

WHEREAS, Lowell Green has been in the pet store business, the ice cream business, the travel business, the farming business, the publishing business, and in fact, has also been a candidate for the Liberal Party of Ontario; and

WHEREAS, at all relevant times Bob Chiarelli shopped at the pet store, ate his ice cream, acted as lawyer to his travel agency, read his books, knocked on doors for him when he was a Liberal candidate (yes, he was—that's no joke!); and

WHEREAS, the talk show audience constantly accuses Lowell Green of favouritism towards the Mayor and the City's management; and

WHEREAS, the Mayor wishes to dispel any idea of favouritism;

THEREFORE, in honour of Lowell Green's 50th anniversary in broadcasting, instead of proclaiming this day "Lowell Green Day" in Ottawa, I, Bob Chiarelli, Mayor of the City of Ottawa, do hereby proclaim this morning "LOWELL GREEN HALF-ASSED DAY" in the City of Ottawa.

Signed: Bob Chiarelli, Mayor, City of Ottawa

• • •

So, you tell me. Should I be honoured or not? I'm still trying to figure it out, but this I have discovered: It is a distinction never before bestowed on anyone in all of Canada. Plenty of people have had a day proclaimed in their honour, but never before has anyone ever had the distinction of having a half-assed day named after them. I am the only person on the face of the planet who can make this claim to fame, a fact pointed out by a fellow tourist as we visited Hollywood's Grauman's Chinese Theatre a few months ago.

"Seems to me," he mused, as we examined the famous footprints that adorn the cement just outside the theatre, "seems to me a famous cheek would fit right in here!"

Lowell's Canada

In his statement of defence to the Canadian Broadcast Standards Council, concerning the "Somalian affair," CFRA News Director Steve Winogron made mention of a series I researched, wrote and broadcast to an extensive radio network in the 1970s and '80s.

The series was featured on more than twenty Canadian radio stations over a period of several years. As I look back now, there is no question they were one of the best-received things I ever did. Dozens of schools requested copies. Unlike most of my programs, we never received a single complaint and almost all mail was laudatory. I have to confess that something else I do when I think back to that series, which we called "Lowell Green's Canada," is recollect that I earned a maximum of $500 or $600 for the entire series of about 150 scripts, despite it taking me the better part of a year to do the research. The stations aside from CFRA paid me $3 for each of the stories designed to be read in 90 seconds. Come to think of it, I don't think CFRA paid me anything for them!

The idea was to present a little bit of Canadian history with a sort of believe-it-or-not twist, featuring every aspect of Canadian life from before the arrival of the white man to something which may have occurred only a few days ago.

For example, here's a story I'll bet you never heard before. It was first broadcast on CFRA on April 11, 1977, as part of the "Lowell Green's Canada" series:

There was once a strange and secret society boasting as many as 150,000 members with the sole purpose of capturing Canada. That story in a moment.

[Insert commercials—which were probably sold for $100 a minute, maybe more.]

They were called the "Patriot Hunters"—a band of men formed in northern Vermont in the spring of 1883. Dozens more "Hunters" lodges sprang up all along the American side of the St. Lawrence Valley, following the abortive rebellions in Upper and Lower Canada.

The Lodges had secret signs, passwords and names for the ranks. The "Snowshoes" were soldiers without rank; "Beavers" were commissioned officers; "Grand Hunters" were field officers; the "Patriot Hunters" were officers of the highest rank.

Elaborate signs and passwords were devised for recognition among "Hunters," and candidates were all required to take an oath stating: "I solemnly swear in the presence of Almighty God that I will not reveal the secret signs of the 'Snowshoes' to anyone, not even members of the Society. I will not write, print, mark, engrave, scratch, chalk or in any conceivable manner make the shape or sign of the 'Snowshoe' to any living being; not even to members of the Society." The oath then went on at some length promising that the new members would reveal any plots against the Society, and so on.

Once the oath had been given, the blindfold was removed to reveal a burning candle, a naked sword pointed at the recruit's heart and two pistols flashed in front of his face. He was promised that his throat would be cut should he in any way fail to live up to his oath.

It was the Hunter Society that organized and financed the disastrous attack at Prescott and the subsequent battle of Windmill Point (you can still see the bullet holes in the windmill!). They also launched another abortive attack at Windsor—both in 1838. But despite the setbacks, the Hunters continued to increase their support—both in the United States and to a certain extent even here in Canada. Their peak seems to have been in 1840 when as many of 150,000 or 160,000 thousand members claimed to belong.

While they didn't have much success in attacking and capturing Canada, for about four years they did force the British to maintain a strong military force along the St. Lawrence and in no small way helped to unite Canada and prepare her for Confederation which followed in a few years.

• • •

Another popular broadcast was the following, which listeners first heard on CFRA January 10, 1997:

It's December 1993. Thousands of people in Canada and the United States are praying for the recovery of one of hockey's greatest stars. Radio stations in both countries are broadcasting hourly bulletins on his condition. A little nurse spends the night slapping his face to keep him awake and alive. Then yet another crisis, solved by a chicken fancier. That story in a moment.

[Commercial. Don't forget I'm not getting any of this. How dumb is that?!]

Ace Bailey, star forward with the Toronto Maple Leafs hovers near death in a Boston hospital, having been checked to the ice a few days before by Eddie Shore in the Boston Gardens.

Radio stations from coast to coast urge everyone to pray for his recovery. His name is on everyone's lips, hockey fans or not. There's no hope for Ace. Plans are made to ship his body back to Canada.

At his bedside is a nurse, recalled by those who were there only as Miss Ahn. Whenever Ace seems to be slipping away, she gently slaps his face and says, "Ace, keep fighting; your team needs you."

Then in the midst of this crisis, Maple Leaf Team Assistant Frank Selke gets a phone call in Toronto. It's Leaf's team owner Conn Smyth. Bailey's father is in a Boston hotel. He's got a gun and swears he's going to get Shore. "Do something," orders Smyth. Selke begins to tick off in his mind the names of everyone he knows in Boston who might be able to help. He recalls a fellow by the name of Bob Huddy, a Boston policeman who, like Selke, raised and showed fancy chickens. "Sure," says Huddy, "glad to help out."

Huddy finds Mr. Bailey, talks him out of his gun, puts him on a train and orders the conductor not to let him off before Toronto.

Ace Bailey makes a miraculous recovery but is never again able to play professional hockey.

• • •

One of my favourite stories is perhaps better known to a few of you, but is so incredible it's worth repeating. It was first broadcast on CFRA in June of 1996:

The assassination of Thomas D'Arcy McGee, April 7, 1868, on Sparks Street in Ottawa was actually only part of a much larger and really incredible story, which I'll tell you in just a moment.

[You know what's here.]

D'Arcy McGee was one of nine Irishmen who were captured and convicted of treason against Her Majesty Queen Victoria for taking part in the Irish rebellion. All were sentenced to die.

The public outcry, however, was so great that the Queen decided to exile them all to Australia instead. McGee, disguised as priest, escaped and somehow made his way to Canada, where within a few years he became a Member of Parliament and one of the Fathers of Confederation. Rather incredibly, the other eight Irishmen convicted of treason also reached positions of great importance. Charles Duffy, for example, later Sir Charles Duffy, became Prime Minister of Australia just 25 years after being exiled there as a penniless prisoner.

And the others? Listen to this: Thomas Meager became Governor of Montana. Terrance McManus ended up as a Brigadier of the United States Army, as did Patrick Donohuse. Richard O'Gorman became Governor of Newfoundland. Morris Lyne became Attorney General of Australia and was succeeded by Michael Ireland, another of the men deported. The last of the nine men convicted of treason, John Mitchell, became a prominent New York politician, the father of New York Mayor Patrick (Paddy) Mitchell, as a matter of fact.

McGee, of course, met a tragic and untimely death at the hands of a murderer in downtown Ottawa, but like the other eight, he made a major contribution to his adopted land.

Thumbnail Sketches of a Few Notable Encounters of the Mic Kind

I've met just about every Canadian, and a few others, worth interviewing over the some 50 years I've been at this radio game. Just for the fun of it, the following is a totally unfair, totally subjective thumb-nail sketch of just a few of the most notable.

FUNNIEST:

Rich Little, who once phoned my show and for several minutes had me convinced it was President Richard Nixon calling to complain about my criticism of Watergate. I should have known better, but Rich was so convincing he even had our entire news department thinking we had a big scoop!

SEXIEST:

Wow! No doubt about it. Diane Francis, editor of the *Financial Post* who showed up in my studio a couple of years ago wearing a skin-tight pair of black leotards and little else. Very hard to concentrate. Why doesn't *my* financial advisor look like this?

WEIRDEST:

A toss-up here between two guys whose names I have long since forgotten, but with acts that still jam up my mind. One guy had me and the audience enthralled for an hour claiming that you could self-diagnose almost any illness by checking your earwax! He billed himself as "the Codfather" because his cure for whatever ails you was heavy doses of cod-liver oil. The other guy who just whacked me out was a psychic who used to appear occasionally and send shivers up my spine with his apparent ability to foretell the future, not of the caller on the line—but one of the callers *waiting* on the line. I only discovered later the calls were all set up, but the guy was so good it was worth a little deceit. I tried a little of the psychic bit myself a couple times until, God help me, some people started to take me seriously!

SHYEST:

Pierre Berton. Pierre, one of our greatest authors, hated the obligatory book tour, and while he struck some people as being stand-offish, I got the impression of an extremely shy man. Mine was one of the few open-line shows he would appear on, because he said he was always asked some intelligent questions.

WACKIEST:

Once again a toss-up, this time between former Ottawa Mayor Charlotte Whitton and the present leader of the Green Party, Elizabeth May. Charlotte used to call my show, scream something about me not knowing what I was talking about, then hang up in my ear. Elizabeth May, who appeared on my show in early 2007, claimed Canada could reduce its energy requirements by 50 percent within a few months without in any way harming individuals or businesses. She then went on to say that if elected to power the Green Party would close down all coal-fired and nuclear-generating stations. This too, she claimed, would not hurt the economy! It doesn't get much wackier than that!

MOST INTELLIGENT:

This is a tough one. You tend to think those who agree with you are smarter than those who do not. But I admitted at the outset that this exercise was going to be strictly subjective, so here goes. It's a dead heat among four people. Mike Duffy: hard to find a guy quicker on his feet than Duff. Steve Madely: he'll love me for this, but I've never met anyone who could seize up a situation faster than Steve. The late Hal Anthony, who rose from a junior clerk in a tiny Saskatchewan bank to the peak of the broadcasting profession strictly on the strength of hard work and superior intelligence.

Hal had more curiosity about everything than anyone I have ever met. In France some years ago, Hal insisted we find out what creatures were digging holes in the backyard of the old farmhouse we were renting. I thought they were field mice, but Hal was right, when we finally flushed one of them out, it wasn't a mouse but the strangest looking little toad I have ever seen. And finally, in the intelligence stakes, former Ottawa Mayor Jackie Holtzman. Here is a tiny woman able to lead armies of men entirely with the force of her personality and intelligence.

DUMBEST:

Oh boy, I've had some doozies in this category, but the first prize has got to go to the Vancouver radio host who recently devoted a half-hour of his morning show to interviewing me about my book *How the granola-crunching, tree-hugging, thug huggers are wrecking our country*, but had no idea who I was or what the book was about. Not only that, he had just started his job as morning host, had received the book and my bio a week prior, but hadn't bothered to read any of it. What a way to start a new job! Doesn't get much dumber than that!

BEST ATHLETE:

This is easy. Russ Jackson, who quarterbacked the Ottawa Rough Riders to Grey Cups in 1960, 1968 and 1969, was named the outstanding player in the CFL in 1963, 1966 and 1969, and won a host of other awards, including Canada's Best Athlete. Russ was inducted into the Canadian Football Hall of Fame in 1973. In recent years, the best athlete I have ever seen has to be Daniel Alfredsson of the Ottawa Senators. Daniel is, in my opinion, the most athletic and most complete hockey player in the world today.

NICEST ATHLETE'S WIFE:

Lois Jackson, Russ's wife, who for two seasons co-hosted a novel radio program with me called "The Kitchen Quarterback Club." Lois was beautiful, full of life and energy, very bright, and one of the best at handling difficult (stupid) phone calls. We had a ball on that show. I remember a caller once asking Lois why Russ kept pulling up his socks on the field. "Well," replied Lois, not missing a beat, "probably because I keep telling him to pull up his socks around the house!" By the way, some radio station should pick up the idea for the Senators. No charge for the suggestion.

NICEST ATHLETE:

Patrick Lalime, former Senators' goaltender, was a real sweetheart of a guy but sadly had trouble seeing flying pucks. But the nicest athlete I ever met has to be Brad Marsh, former Ottawa Senator and now owner of Marshy's restaurants. This guy has a heart of gold. The day after listeners donated more than $100,000 during the "Aid for Aiden" campaign, Marshy showed up at the station with $750 in small bills he had collected from his customers and wanted no publicity for it.

BEST SPORTS TEAM:

This is easy. The CFRA Happy Blunderers, who for nearly two decades in the 1960s and '70s took on all challengers up and down the Ottawa and Seaway Valleys, beating them all. If you believe that, you'll believe anything! But we did raise well over $4 million for various charities and causes, entertained thousands of people and had incredible adventures, including learning to slide into a cow pie, which served as second base in Lanark, and losing our centre fielder Chuck Collins in a deep ditch in Chelsea!

THE GUYS I DISAGREED WITH THE MOST:

No contest here. Bob Rae, when he was Premier of Ontario, after I dubbed him Buffalo Bob in honour of all the Ontario businesses fleeing his policies to set up shop in Buffalo. We disagreed so vehemently during an interview on CFRB in Toronto that I suggested it might be best if he just played the piano for the last few minutes of the program. Bob plays a mean piano. Second on this list, no surprise here, Jack Layton. During a half-hour interview on the CFRA program "The Lunch Bunch" recently, I pinned him to the wall, to the mat, to the ceiling, to anything handy. When it was all over, Jack opined that he'd never had an interview like that in his life. To which I say, way to go, Lowell!

THE GUY WHO STILL OWES ME THE MOST MONEY:

Every time I see Henry Champ on CBC Television reporting from Washington, I yell at the screen: "Henry, you still owe me for that guinea pig!" Henry, of course, doesn't hear me and even if he did, knowing Henry, he'd sweet-talk me out of it anyway. Henry Champ and I were good friends when he worked for CFRA in the early to mid-'60s, so it was only natural that he drop into our Little Farm Pet Shop on Sparks Street one day to pick up a guinea pig and cage for one of his children. Notice I didn't say buy. Henry, in those days, never seemed to have any money on him. I figured his credit was good and it probably would have been, except a few weeks later Henry accepted a better paying job someplace and took off with his family, the guinea pig and the cage. So Henry, if you read this, I figure that with interest you now owe me enough for a plane fare down to Washington so you can introduce me to George Bush! I talked with Henry during CFRA's 60th anniversary broadcast in April 2007 and reminded him of his debt. Henry remembered it well and offered to take me to the Washington Press Club for lunch in payment. I'm going to take him up on it!

MOST INTERESTING STORY:

Eugene Whelan, former Minister of Agriculture, came on my show a few years ago to claim that it was he, not Ronald Reagan, who convinced Mikhail Gorbachev to raise the Iron Curtain and abandon communism in the Soviet Union. Whelan makes a powerful case, because it was he who invited Gorbachev to visit Canada in 1984, the Russian's first trip to a non-communist country.

On May 29, 1984, Gorbachev, who was then in the Soviet Politburo responsible for State Agriculture, came to Windsor to have a look at Whelan's Essex County farm. According to Whelan, he and Gorbachev were able to extract themselves from bodyguards and "minders" for a private stroll along the back of his farm where Whelan explained how Canadian farmers operated independent of State control. "Gorbachev," Whelan told me, "could hardly believe how prosperous and well equipped the farm was."

Whelan then convinced the Russians to visit a nearby supermarket with its huge display of fresh produce. "Don't forget," said Whelan, "at this time housewives were lining up for hours to buy a loaf of bread back in Moscow, and here in Canada we were featuring truckloads of every kind of food you could imagine."

At first, Gorbachev thinks it is all a set-up, that the Canadians have deliberately arranged this display for his benefit. "Okay," says Whelan, "let's get into your limo. You point any direction and we'll drive until we find another supermarket!" Sure enough, a couple of miles away they come upon a huge Loblaws, even larger than the first. "Gorbachev was stunned, absolutely stunned," Whelan told me. "That's when I think he first realized that the communist system just didn't stand a chance against capitalism. You could see it in his eyes! There's absolutely no question in my mind that it was that day which convinced Gorbachev that if he ever had the chance, he would end communism and institute a system that actually fed the people!"

THE NICEST:

I still say it has to be Tommy Douglas, who could not have been kinder to a young and very green rookie during my first live broadcast from Parliament Hill in 1960. A close second would be former Ottawa City Controller and Speaker of the House of Commons, the late Lloyd Francis. A very kind, intelligent, well-informed gentleman, Lloyd helped me out many times during my early days at CFRA when I was covering City Hall.

MOST FASCINATING CHARACTER:

Colonel Saunders of Kentucky Fried Chicken fame. He marched into my studio in full regalia—stark white tropical suit, top to bottom, sporting his famous cane. He enthralled us all for a solid hour, boasting that he had gone bankrupt 12 times before he finally hit pay dirt. "If you haven't hit the canvas a few times in your life," he suggested, "you just aren't trying hard enough. Most of us waste our lives by playing things far too safe. Hell's bells, if Columbus and all those guys in those old wooden ships hadn't set out over what they feared would be the edge of the world, we'd still all be jammed into Italy!"

THE SCARIEST:

It's shortly after my show several years ago when I look up to see a big brute of a man, sporting tattoos and a straggly pigtail halfway down his back, wander into the newsroom looking like he's ready to blow up the place. I know immediately who it is—Andre the Bomber, a frequent caller to my show, whose claim to fame is he's spent several years in prison for setting off a bomb near a Montreal school during the FLQ crisis. Fearing he might be packing a bomb again, I grab him by the arm and hustle him out of the crowded newsroom into our main lobby. Suffering a severe brain cramp, or maybe just forgetting exactly how old I am, I slap my hands together, bounce into my best version of the Mohammed Ali stance, and say, "LET'S GO!" (Honest to God, I was that nuts.) Andre stops dead in his tracks, looking stunned, and then turns on his heel and walks out of the station. A couple of weeks later, he writes me a scrawled letter in which he proclaims, "I've been shot at, stabbed, hit with a baseball bat and a lead pipe, but I've never had anyone slap his hands and say, 'Let's go!'" I never heard from him again. We immediately installed some security at the station!

BEST VOCABULARY:

John Diefenbaker. No question. The Chief had full command of every word Oxford ever dreamed up and wasn't averse to using them all. In fact, I think he invented a few words not in the dictionary during a 15-minute heated tongue-lashing he laid on me one day when I mistakenly claimed that his wife, Olive, was a divorced woman, not a widowed one.

BEST ON-AIR DRINKER:

Farley Mowatt, head and shoulders above all contenders. A 24-ouncer of rum and a pitcher of ice water down the hatch in an hour-and-a-half program! Not bad for a little guy. Amazingly, even after that workout, he was still able to talk, and sometimes actually make sense!

MOST ARROGANT:

Look up the word in your dictionary and you'll see a picture of the guy, beard and all. David Suzuki is way out in front in this category. No interest in me, my opinions, or anyone who called. Just wanted to make it very clear I was bloody lucky to have him on my show so he could push his latest book! Actually, Pierre Trudeau wasn't exactly the most humble of men, although in a private phone call to me, he did express gratitude for my criticism of reporters who had been sneaking around hospital corridors stalking Margaret when she was having mental health problems. Pierre even sent me a very complimentary letter when I first retired from CFRA in 1978.

HANDSOMEST:

You aren't going to believe this, but according to almost all women who ever saw him, the best-looking man I ever interviewed was former *Toronto Sun* "Sunshine Boy" Alexander McQuirter, Grand Wizard of the KKK! I'm not making this up. The guy was a bona fide fruitcake and white supremacist, but he had women in the station swooning. No question this guy could have been a big-time Hollywood star if he wasn't such a nutcase. Come to think of it, as a nutcase, McQuirter should have fit right in with that Beverly Hills crowd! Perhaps he just wasn't crazy enough! Or maybe the fact that he was convicted of hiring a hit man to kill a rival Klan member was just a bit too much even for Hollywood!

BEST NUTTY AS A FRUITCAKE STATEMENT:

Left-wing Ottawa City Councillor Alex Cullen takes the cake here. Famous for warning us not to put those new low-energy light bulbs in the "Carp Mountain" or any other dump because the mercury might leak out and pollute the land, all the while reassuring us that the dumps aren't a danger to us since nothing could leak out of them. Go figure.

BEST STAND-UP COMIC:

You haven't seen a really hilarious comedy act until you've seen J. J. Clarke do his nasty Santa Claus routine. I was wondering if I had made a mistake in signing on with CKOY (now Oldies 1310) when they invited me to a Christmas party at the Silver Dollar strip club on Merivale Road, but J. J.'s Santa Claus act, in full Santa regalia, convinced me that anyone that funny had to be a big winner. On the other hand, the fact CKOY held its Christmas party at a strip club should have set off an alarm bell if I'd been a bit smarter!

MOST ANNOYING:

No doubt about it, Jay the Socialist. Thank goodness the Liberals finally hired this guy and gave him something to do other than drive me crazy, although every once in a while he seems to crop up again, like a socialist heading for the trough! By the way, the next person who calls me their "favourite dinosaur" gets to job-share with Jay for a month!

BEST DUPE JOB:

I have long since forgotten his name but after an appearance on "The Greenline" during which he talked about the "troubles" in Ireland, I learned he was a recruiter and fundraiser for the IRA. He was a great charmer and kisser of the Blarney Stone, and I suspect he had a little fling with one of our female employees.

BEST SOLDIER:

No doubt about it. Rick Hillier, Chief of Defence Staff. Not afraid to take on anyone, including the Liberals, but a very accomplished diplomat, as well. We saw evidence of that during the Lowell Green Roast in April 2006. Several of the ladies (I'm a gentleman and won't tell you who) at Rick's table, after several rounds of "good cheer," began calling him Ricky and other terms of endearment, and he never even flinched! Wonderful grace under fire.

BEST SPORT:

You aren't going to believe this, but I've got to hand this award to the Premier of Ontario, Dalton McGuinty. Despite everything I've ever said about this guy, he was enough of a really good sport to record one of the funniest bits we heard during the aforementioned Lowell Green Roast. His line about mistaking me for Lorne Green got one of the biggest laughs of the night.

RICHEST GUY I EVER TURNED DOWN:

When famous talk-show host Jack Webster left CKNW Vancouver in 1972, Jim Pattison, who even then was one of the richest and nicest men in Canada, came to Ottawa to try to convince me to head west and take over what Jack had left. Jim's promises were considerable: a lot more money than I was earning and a house in North Vancouver. Kitty and I had just bought a little island cottage in the Thousand Islands and we couldn't bring ourselves to leave. Jim was genuinely astonished at the turndown, but never held it against me. I met him several times after that and each time he would always wink and say, "That North Van house is still waiting for you."

BEST NEGOTIATOR:

Has to be former CFRA General Manager and sportscaster par excellence Terry Kielty. Immediately after the offer from Jim Pattison, I thought I should be able to crank it to CFRA pretty good. By the time I got through with Terry, it's a wonder I wasn't thanking him for not reducing my salary. Well, that's a bit of an exaggeration, but if Pattison ever found out how little I settled for, it wouldn't be a house he'd have ready for me, but the guys with a butterfly net!

BIGGEST HEART:

Could we have anyone other than entrepreneur, community leader and philanthropist Dave Smith win in this category? Is there any charitable endeavour Dave doesn't help or is willing to? From skates for kids in the far north to health supplies for Africans, Dave is there. I can honestly say every time any organization I ever worked with needed some help, Dave Smith was the guy you called. Believe me, there are probably hundreds of other people in Ottawa and the Valley who could tell you the same thing. I wasn't so crazy about Dave the first time I met him however. He beat me so badly in the racquetball court, I sulked for a week.

BEST PLAY-BY-PLAY ANNOUNCER:

My old friend Dean Brown does a fine job as play-by-play man for the Ottawa Senators, Ernie Calcutt was one of the finest when he called Ottawa Rough Riders games, but there is no one better at bringing the excitement of a game into your living room than Dave (Voice, as in the voice of the Ottawa 67's) Schreiber. His best line has to be when a 67's player shoots one just under the crossbar into the opposing net, and Voice screams, "HE FIRES ONE TOP SHELF— WHERE GRANDMAW KEEPS THE HOMEMADE JAM!"

MOST DESCRIPTIVE PLAY-BY-PLAY CALL:

Not much question here. Several years ago, the Ottawa Senators, I think playing the New Jersey Devils. Daniel Alfredsson scores after being deposited onto the seat of his pants with Dean Brown screaming: "SCORES! ALFREDSSON KNOCKS THE PUCK INTO THE NET FROM THE TOBOGGAN POSITION!" Priceless!

SMARTEST RADIO EXECUTIVE:
Mark Maheu, former General Manager of CHUM operations in Ottawa. He hired me to host "The Lowell Green Show." Nuff said?!

SECOND SMARTEST RADIO EXECUTIVE:
CFRA Program Director Dave Mitchell, who after a bad day on the show soothes me with mincemeat tarts from Grahame's Bakery in Kemptville.

The Unexplained

I don't believe in angels. I don't believe in any aspect of the paranormal. My wife, Deborah, on the other hand, is steadfast in her belief that given the lifestyle I've led and all the risks I've taken over the years, the fact I am still alive is proof that at least one angel has been assigned to me. Maybe more. It is one of those angels, she claims, who pointed me to her! I laugh when she makes the claim and yet, *and yet*, there are two instances in my life for which I can find no "logical" explanation.

There was certainly an angel of some kind involved when the fan belt on my '56 Meteor broke in the dead of winter in the middle of nowhere. It's about 2:00 a.m., February 2, 1957, on one of the most desolate stretches of road in Canada at the time—Highway 17 between Deep River and North Bay. I'm racing back from a Montreal weekend to my job with CKSO-TV in Sudbury. As usual, I'm running late and have the Meteor whipped up to a good 70 or 80 mph when there's a pop under the hood, a horrible flapping noise and a sudden plume of steam. Busted fan belt!

It's at least 50 miles to the nearest town; there hasn't been another car on the road for the past half-hour, maybe longer, and the temperature outside hovers well below zero. In short, I'm in mighty big trouble! I have none of the things you're supposed to have when driving in remote areas. No blanket, no candles, heck, I don't even have a shovel with which to start building an igloo! Another ten minutes and I figure I'll start writing my will, except I can't find a pen.

Here's where it gets really weird. I'm on a flat stretch of road, so I should be able to see an approaching car from either direction at least a mile or so away, but from nowhere a set of car lights suddenly whips in behind me. A young man gets out. "Thank heavens," or something like that, I say with great relief. "I thought I was going to die here. My fan belt broke."

"Ah," he says, "that's not a problem."

As God is my witness, he goes back to his car, pulls a fan belt and a wrench out of his trunk, and in less than five minutes has the belt on and the motor purring along perfectly. He drops the hood, smiles and before I can really thank him, he's gone. I want to at least offer to pay something, so I take off after him. But just as mysteriously as he appeared he has now disappeared into the night. I crank the Meteor up to nearly 90 in hopes of overtaking him. Nothing! Only the dark, the cold and the lightly drifting snow. As I pull into North Bay, I realize I am singing to myself.

The rest of the car has pretty well fallen apart when I finally sell it three years later, but the fan belt? Still humming along like new!

Who was that mysterious man? How did he happen to have a fan belt that fit my car? Where did he come from? What was he doing driving that lonely stretch of road that late at night? Where did he go? Who, other than my wife, can explain it? Some 50 years later it still gives me goosebumps to think about it!

• • •

A second "unexplained" is, in some ways, even stranger.

It's 1980, my marriage of 19 years is over, I haven't as yet met Deborah, interest rates of nearly 20 percent threaten the travel agency my partners and I have launched, I'm living in an ancient one bed-room apartment with what looks to be thousand-year-old furniture, life is about as bad as it gets, so in anguish I flee to Freeport, Grand Bahama, for a few days to lick my wounds.

And there I have one of the most graphic dreams of my life. At least I presume it was a dream! In it, I meet a beautiful blond-haired woman named Rose Simpson. Let me make it very clear I had never known a Rose Simpson, didn't know anyone who knew a Rose Simpson, and as a matter of fact didn't know anyone named Rose. Even stranger, I cannot recall ever having a dream before or since which invented a name. It was a dream that had such a profound effect on me, seemed so real, that I spent much of the day walking around in a kind of daze.

Desperate to shake the mood and hoping to spot some friends that night, I drive to the local casino, wander around for about an hour, play a few hands of blackjack, and then for some inexplicable reason head for the roulette table. Why I would do this I have no idea, since I believe roulette is a mug's game played only by James Bond and hon-eymooners so satiated with sex their brains are slipping gears. Who's sitting at the table, idly playing with a small pile of chips, is no mug, and since there doesn't appear to be an accompanying male, she's obviously not on honeymoon and, believe me, she's no James Bond. Miss Moneypenny maybe! Slim, very attractive with long blond, almost white hair, spilling well below her shoulders. One cool lady!

I join the table, hoping…well you never know, do you? She glances my way a couple times, but after dropping too many bucks, I give it up and head back to a lonely bed, kicking myself for not bucking up a bit more courage and doing something a bit more productive than making a donation to the casino's sucker fund.

Things pick up the next day when I team up with two young guys on the golf course and manage to win back a few dollars lost the night before. We have a couple of after-game drinks and I offer to drive them back to their hotel since they've come by cab. They're staying at the Xanadu Hotel, famous as the place Howard Hughes built and then holed up in as a crazy man during the last years of his life. The beach at the Xanadu is one of the poorest on the island, narrow and always overcrowded. I hadn't been there for years, but for some reason I decide that I'll take a dip there after dropping off my golf buddies, so on the way, I stop off at my little hideaway, don a bathing suit and head for a date with destiny.

After arranging another golf date for the next day with my new buddies, I stroll down the beach and there she is! Still slim, still beautiful with her long blond hair tied back with a gay bandana. She's sitting alone under her umbrella so I take the plunge.

"How'd you make out at the casino last night?" She looks up at me with a slight smile. "I saw you there last night, how did you do?" I laugh and make some inane remark about fools and their money soon being parted and squat down on my haunches beside her. We do the usual little dance. She's from New York, down for a week. "I'm from Ottawa, ever hear of it, ha, ha?"

Time to give it the test. "Think I'll take a little dip," I say and stand up. She jumps to her feet. "Mind if I join you?" "Of course not," is what I say. What I'm thinking is. "YES, there really is a God!"

I've pushed the reset button in my mind countless times on this one and the picture never varies and never ceases to spook me.

I'm standing up to my neck in the beautiful warm blue waters of the Bahamas beneath a polished sky. She's a couple of feet closer to shore facing me, squinting slightly into the sun. A stray strand of wet hair is plastered to a cheekbone; her breasts stir with each gentle wave.

"Guess I should introduce myself," I say, "my name's Lowell." She smiles, brushes away the stray hair. "My name's Rose."

I must have gone white because she looks anxious for a moment, and puzzled. "Are you all right?"

I shake it off with a laugh, but in fact my knees feel about to buckle.

It is all so weird I never did tell her why I was so anxious to get back to some solid footing on shore that day.

Her last name wasn't Simpson, which is probably a good thing since that would have been just too much for anyone to believe. She was a successful surgeon from New York. It never developed into anything very serious, but we enjoyed each other's company very much. She introduced me to parts of New York City that I would otherwise never have seen. For awhile she tried to convince me to take a job with a New York radio station and even lined up an interview for me with WNEW. I was tempted, but less than a week before the scheduled audition, I met Deborah and nothing, not even a job with New York's leading radio station, could persuade me to leave Ottawa and the woman I knew, even then, I was going to marry.

Rose and I said goodbye to each other over dinner at Windows of the World, on the 106th and 107th floors of the North Tower of the World Trade Center.

The "Perfect" Flood

From this valley they say you are going
We will miss your bright eyes and sweet smile
For they say you are taking the sunshine
That has brightened our pathway awhile

Come and sit by my side if you love me
Do not hasten to bid me adieu
But remember the Red River Valley
And the one who has loved you so true

(Popular 19th century folk song)

The plane banks slightly as we approach the Winnipeg airport and we see it. An enormous inland sea. More than two thousand square miles of muddy water stretching from well below the American border to the southern suburbs of Winnipeg—the "Red Sea!" In its path a dike that resembles the Great Wall of China, zigzagging for nearly 40 miles across the Manitoba prairie. Dozens of what, from this height, look like toy trucks, bulldozers, cranes and even helicopters swarm over and around it. Steve Madely and I have been told completion of the dike is a race against time.

What we can see being feverishly built far below us is the vital Brunkild Dike, commonly called the Z-Dike because of the manner in which it zigzags across the landscape. If it isn't completed before the flood waters from the rampaging Red River reach it in another 24 to 36 hours, or if fails to hold back the advancing waters, now more than nine feet deep in places, the entire City of Winnipeg and most of its

650,000 citizens may have to be evacuated. The damage would be incalculable.

The main problem with the Red River is that it flows north. As the spring melt generally starts in the south and works its way gradually north, it means that while the southern portion of the river is gorged from melting snow, the ice has not as yet cleared away from the northern part of the river, preventing it from flowing swiftly into Lake Winnipeg.

This happens almost every year to some degree, but there were additional factors that caused the great flood of 1950 and the one Steve Madely and I covered for CFRA in the spring of 1997.

The flood of the century, as the 1997 flood is now called, actually began with record rainfall in the fall of 1996, saturating the ground until it couldn't absorb any more water. Adding to the problem, helping to create, if you like, "the perfect flood" was record cold during the winter. From November 7, 1996 until March 18, 1997 (a total of 131 days), the temperature only reached 40 degrees Fahrenheit for three days in the City of Grand Forks, North Dakota, on the banks of the Red River well to the south of Winnipeg. This then didn't allow for any gradual melting, but on March 19, 1997, the temperature rose above freezing for 27 consecutive days. The sudden warmth melted the snow pack too quickly for the river to handle. To make things even worse, a freak blizzard hit the southern portion of the Red River Valley on April 5.

The result was the worst flooding of the Red River since 1950. It would have been an unprecedented tragedy were it not for the foresight of former Manitoba Premier Duff Roblin, who convinced the government of the day to dig a huge ditch, ringing the City of Winnipeg. Called either Duff's Ditch or Roblin's Folly, depending upon your politics, it taps into the Red River to the south of the city, skirts around Winnipeg's eastern edge for more than 47 kilometres, and then empties back into the river well to the north. Started in 1962 and completed

Thousands of Winnipeg volunteers sandbag the famous Z-Dike that saved the city from devastation during the great Winnipeg flood of 1997. Steve Madely and I were there bringing the drama into the homes of thousands of concerned listeners in Ottawa and the region. CFRA listeners donated well over $100,000 for flood relief.

Steve Madely brings my listeners up-to-date from the banks of the huge inland sea created by the floodwaters of the rampaging Red River.

four years later at a cost of $63 million, it has a minimum depth of 24 feet and can bleed off a tremendous volume of water. It was extremely controversial while being built, but when Steve and I arrive in Winnipeg with flood waters threatening to engulf the city, there isn't a soul who doesn't agree it's the only thing preventing a complete disaster.

Just about everyone I speak with during the time we spend in Winnipeg says the same thing when asked what they think of Duff's Ditch now. "A godsend," is the most common reply.

How right they are! Even as our plane is landing the evening of April 30, white-capped waves, whipped up by high winds, are smashing through the dikes encircling the village of Ste-Agathe only a few miles south of Winnipeg. All residents of that community are being evacuated, with thousands of others from Winnipeg all the way south to the US border, ordered to be ready to evacuate within 24 hours. More than 15,000 people have already been forced to leave their homes and farms. The cities of Grand Forks, North Dakota, and East Grand

Forks, Minnesota, have both been completely submerged by the river which peaked at an incredible 49 feet, more than 20 feet above flood level. Damage in the twin cities exceeds $2 billion.

Residents of Winnipeg are expecting the worst. More than four million sandbags have been produced by the time we arrive and now line the dikes protecting the centre of the city. A huge army of volunteers, working in shifts around the clock, is making an incredible 300,000 sandbags a day. Every manhole in the entire city is either covered with sandbags to prevent sewers from backing up, or has a nearby pile ready to apply.

In my first broadcast back to Ottawa the night we arrive, I describe the mood in Winnipeg as calm but fearful. Their hopes are pinned on two things: Duff's Ditch and the Z-Dike. As I am broadcasting, Duff's Ditch, officially named the Floodway, is diverting 60,000 cubic feet of water a second around the city. When you consider that the river itself is moving 75,000 cubic feet of water a second, you can understand how vital the ditch is and what would happen had it not been built.

But even Duff's Ditch can't save the city if they can't complete the Z-Dike in time or if it doesn't hold against nine-foot-deep flood waters that are slowly rolling toward it.

Why was the construction of the Z-Dike left so late? I've asked the question repeatedly and never received what I consider a satisfactory answer. Was it a failure to understand the magnitude of the flood waters approaching Winnipeg? Was it a failure to understand the topography of the surrounding countryside? Was it overconfidence in Duff's Ditch, or just plain and simple incompetence? I suspect a bit of all the aforementioned.

Here is the threat that, incredibly, was only realized at the last moment. If you examine a map of the area, you will see that the LaSalle River drains the area to the west of the Red River and enters the Red River just to the north of not only Winnipeg's diking system, but most importantly, the La Salle River enters the Red River just to the north of Duff's Ditch. If the floodwaters slowly but inexorably approaching Winnipeg from the west hit the LaSalle River, it will create a raging torrent aimed directly at the heart of the city past the dikes and the ditch. The perfect end run to disaster!

For some reason, the danger is only identified three days before the flood is predicted to reach the banks of the LaSalle River. Clearly another massive dike has to be constructed to prevent the giant sea from reaching the LaSalle. But where should the dike be built? How can it be built in 72 hours? And can a dike built in that short space of time be high enough and strong enough to hold back the approaching sea?

A private survey company, with the aid of satellites, quickly identifies the best path, taking into account existing roads and railways, hills, fences, and so on.

More than eight thousand men, many of them members of Canada's military based at Camp Petawawa, then begin what becomes the largest military operation since the Korean War. Called Operation Assistance, it is the largest peacetime military operation in Canada's history.

The dike is being built out of whatever the workers can get their hands on. Some parts are made from prairie gumbo, taken straight from farmer's fields by backhoes, and then packed into the dike by bulldozers. Other parts are built from limestone that is trucked in from nearby quarries. Another section is built from huge sandbags, weighing nearly three thousand pounds, dropped into place by cranes. The army adds 27,000 feet of oil boom. The army's Griffin helicopters dropping 130-foot-long phosphorous flames, each with the power of two million candles, illuminates night operations. Work must not be halted, even for a moment. Time is running out. The mighty "Red Sea" grows closer by the minute.

There are reports that old car and bus bodies are being jammed into the dike, but in fact, that's not quite true. Large pieces of junk, including car and bus bodies, were dropped into areas to the south of the dike in hopes they might help lessen the wave action pounding into the dike itself. This, by the way, worked quite effectively.

One of the most difficult tasks in broadcasting something of this magnitude is absorbing all the information piling into your head from a myriad of sources, some reliable, some not so. As you can imagine, in situations of this nature, rumours, rumours of rumours, and outright lies abound. Within a few hours of arriving and while on a tour of the city, we were informed that the Village of St. Norbert had been wiped from the face of the map by the encroaching sea. Subsequent investigation reveals this to be untrue, although Ste. Agathe is being inundated. We are also told that consideration is being given to closing the gates to Duff's Ditch and allowing Winnipeg to flood because residents to the south are complaining they are being sacrificed in order to save the Manitoba capital. The stories of complaints from some were certainly true, as we later learned, but there was never a serious thought about closing the gates leading into the ditch or breaching the dikes in order to flood Winnipeg and alleviate the flood backing up behind them to the south.

It was also extremely difficult to determine progress on the Z-Dike. If this had been in Ottawa, both Steve and I would have established sources we could contact and trust, but here in a strange city in the grip of fear, reliable information is at a premium. We manage to track down a good contact in a position of command in Petawawa, and through him we keep our listeners better informed about the progress of the vital dike than the local media in Winnipeg are able to do. It is from this source that Steve and I are among the first, if not the very first, to express the military's belief that the dike will be completed in time to halt the approaching flood tide and that they have every reason to believe it will hold fast.

What strikes both Steve and me the evening we arrive is the calmness of the city. We tour from one end of Winnipeg to the other, even crossing the surging Red River to St. Boniface. What we need in order to paint a proper picture for our listeners is an overall view of not only the actual flooding, but also the manner in which Winnipegers are dealing with it. We need a good look and a thorough understanding of the enemy and how it is being fought. One of the first things we notice is that with few exceptions the "Red Sea" is, thus far, being successfully held at bay. Aside from the piled sandbags at all the storm sewer catch basins, the frantic volunteer workforce working around the clock making sandbags in a large arena, and trucks hauling the bags away, there is little evidence of the danger that lurks just outside the dikes.

"I wonder if the Romans were this calm with the barbarians at their gates as Winnipegers are with the sea at their dikes," I remark to Steve as our progress south along Pembina Street is halted by one of the dikes protecting the city. Boats are moored to the pillars of a highway overpass as three- and four-foot waves lap at the outer edges of the dike. Fate has decided that the hotel booked for us is only about a block from the sea and the dike, and as we register we are informed by the desk clerk that if the dike breaks during the night, we will immediately be notified and will have less than half an hour to evacuate. He acts as though this is more or less a routine occurrence.

The first thing I do when I awake the next morning is check to see if it's a boat or car we need to make our way to Winnipeg's most famous landmark, The Forks. Thank heavens, the dike is still holding. A boat isn't needed.

But if the water rises another few inches, they'll need boats to evacuate the stores, restaurants, huge marketplace building and theatres that circle the huge plaza called The Forks, the cultural and entertainment centre of Winnipeg, and the heart and soul of the city. (Those of you who have visited there know it's called The Forks because it's where the two great rivers—the Red and the Assiniboine—meet.)

As we set up for the 6:00 a.m. (5:00 a.m. Winnipeg time) start of Steve Madely's live broadcast on CFRA in Ottawa, the confluence of the rivers is an enormous, angry, boiling cauldron that threatens to march up the final two steps of the broad stone pathway that, in calmer times, leads from the plaza down to the water's edge some 20 feet below. This morning the water's edge is a mere 11 inches from spilling over the steps onto the plaza and into the heart of the city. If it spills over the steps, it means that it is also spilling over many of the dikes and embankments that line the river. You cannot see what is happening here without your heart beating faster. If the Z-Dike cannot hold back the waters from reaching the LaSalle River only a few miles to the south of where we now stand, all the sandbags in the world will not save Winnipeg!

Steve does a marvelous job of painting the grim picture to his listeners back in Ottawa. I have researched the situation with the Z-Dike and bring listeners up-to-date. We also talk about the fundraising effort underway in Manitoba, and speak with representatives of both the Red Cross and the Salvation Army who are raising millions for the disaster fund. I report that more than 20,000 people have now been evacuated south of Winnipeg, about 5,000 overnight, with more likely forced to leave their homes before I begin my program at 9:00 a.m. Ottawa time. Steve interviews Doctor Jim Peplow, the Manitoba Medical Officer of Health, and Don Rocon, a Manitoba drinking-water expert. Both are very concerned about the possibility of downtown flooding, but reassure us that, as of now, the city and its drinking water are safe.

I remain at The Forks to do my show while Steve boards a small boat to be ferried to the Z-Dike where he reports back to me via his cellphone on the progress being made. The flood waters by now are estimated to be less than 24 hours away from the dike, with a great deal of work yet to be completed before it is both high and strong enough to withstand the pounding waves now reported to be more than four feet high.

"We've said it many times, we say it again," says Steve, "it's a race against time. It is going to be very close, but the equipment, the manpower and the organization we see here at work on this tremendous project are truly astonishing."

Meantime, I learn that the Red River and the Assiniboine are expected to crest in downtown Winnipeg sometime early tomorrow afternoon, that is Friday, May 2. The drama mounts. As Manitoba Premier Gary Filmon comments, "it's white knuckle time." The dikes along the Red and Assiniboine Rivers in the heart of Winnipeg will be severely tested as the rivers crest, while several miles to the south, the "Red Sea" is expected to begin to challenge the Z-Dike. "Tomorrow will tell the tale," says the Premier. "If the dikes hold, Winnipeg will be safe. If either of the dikes are breached it could be very serious." He avoids using stronger terms, but most residents of the city understand very well what he means and make preparations to evacuate quickly. But there is a growing belief that, thanks to the dikes and Duff's Ditch, Winnipeg will be spared the worst.

That afternoon, I complete my show in Ottawa, then co-host the afternoon talk show on CJOB, Winnipeg. I tell listeners I am very impressed with the calm courage they are displaying and the fact that thousands of them—men, women and even school children—are volunteering their services night and day to make sandbags and to work on the dikes. Callers express appreciation for the tremendous support and assistance they are receiving from right across the country. "Thus far," I am able to tell them, "about ten million dollars have been donated to the Red Cross; the Salvation Army reports another four million in aid. This is in addition to about $11 million already received in private and corporate donations, including well over $130,000 pledged from CFRA listeners."

Steve and I tour the city and its dikes once again after our shows, check with progress on the Z-Dike, and then turn in for the night close to midnight at our still-dry hotel. Tomorrow we do it all over again at The Forks where we will mount a special flood watch as the rivers crest and the Z-Dike is tested.

Our special guest for the first part of Steve's show the next morning is Winnipeg Mayor Susan Thompson, who dons a brave face but cannot help from time to time anxiously glancing at the roaring, swirling, bubbling tumult of muddy water rushing past us only a few feet away.

During a newsbreak, the Mayor and I peer over the edge of the plaza at the threatening waters below. We are both relieved to see that the level is about the same as it was when last I checked at about 10:00 the night before. If anything, it appears the level may actually have dropped a tiny bit. The Mayor and I look at each other. She smiles. "I think we're going to win this one," she says. There are tears in her eyes.

Steve and I remain broadcasting at The Forks until, at about 2:00 p.m., we get word that the Red River appears to have crested without any serious breaks in city dikes. Even more heartening, the Z-Dike is withstanding everything the "Red Sea" can hurl at it. The sad news is that another 8,000 people south of Winnipeg have had to be evacuated, and while the Z-Dike may very well save Winnipeg, the water, thus backed up, threatens to inundate more communities.

With the imminent danger in Winnipeg over for the time being,

Steve once again is ferried by boat to various flooded communities, conducting interviews and seeing first-hand the terrible devastation. I drive to the local CTV studios where I film a special segment on the flood for "Sunday Edition" with Mike Duffy.

Now assured that the worst is over, Steve and I fly back to Ottawa that night in order to take part in CFRA's 50th anniversary programming the next day. Fittingly enough, it pours rain all that Saturday in Ottawa, and by the time we finish broadcasting from a large tent outside our studios, both Steve and I are soaked through and through. We both laugh at the irony.

At its peak, the "Red Sea" stretched from well south of the American border to the suburbs of Winnipeg, a distance of 110 miles, covering more than two thousand square miles. Eight hundred farms were totally submersed, in some cases covered by nine feet of water. About 28,000 people fled their homes, including about 5,000 in Winnipeg itself, although those in the city proper were evacuated mostly for precautionary reasons. Damage in Winnipeg itself was pretty well restricted to flooded basements in some of the southern communities.

It is estimated that as many as 20,000 civilians took part in sandbag and dike operations, in addition to more than eight thousand soldiers, most of them from Camp Petawawa. In fact, more Canadian soldiers fought the "Red Sea" than the combined strength of the country's peacekeepers in Bosnia, Haiti and the Golan Heights. Four times more soldiers, sailors and airmen took part in saving Winnipeg than are now involved in operations in Afghanistan.

Total damage in Canada is believed to be close to a billion dollars, while destruction just south of the border in Grand Forks and East Grand Forks was in excess of two billion dollars.

Grand Forks didn't have a Duff's Ditch or a giant Z-Dike!

The Great Ice Storm of '98

It's a triple whammy. A huge river of warm, moist air flowing north from the Gulf of Mexico up the Ohio Valley. A massive floating island of cold air, hovering stationary over the St. Lawrence River Valley. And the third ingredient in this recipe for disaster: a high-pressure area like a giant wall, anchored firmly over Bermuda in the central Atlantic— a Bermuda high.

Shortly after midnight on January 5, 1998, the leading edge of the warm moist air begins to slowly attack the cold air mass covering an area stretching roughly from Kingston in Eastern Ontario to Sherbrooke, in the Eastern Townships of Quebec. When warm air meets cold air, the warm air rises over the cold until, in the upper reaches of the atmosphere, the water vapour in the warm air begins to cool and form clouds. The vapour condenses and forms ice crystals, which when they become heavy enough, begin to fall. As they pass through the lower layer of warm air, they melt to form rain. Then, as they continue to fall, they pass through the lower layer of cold air and become supercooled, but for a reason no one has ever been able to explain to me, they still remain in liquid form even though their temperature is well below freezing. This can spell disaster, since the moment this supercooled rain hits any cold object, it freezes instantly.

Those of us who live in or near the Ottawa and St. Lawrence Valleys are no strangers to freezing rain. We usually get a bout or two of it each winter. Ordinarily it lasts only a few hours, and then, as is the case with most weather systems, it all moves eastward, finally dissipating over the North Atlantic.

But not this time. The Bermuda high keeps the whole system

stationary for five full days over Northern New York State, Eastern Ontario and Western Quebec. Tens of thousands of people are also affected in Maine, New Hampshire, Vermont, New Brunswick and Nova Scotia, although by far the hardest hit are Eastern Ontario and Western Quebec, where freezing rain falls almost steadily for a solid 80 hours. Ice as thick as three and four inches is commonplace.

The result is the worst ice storm of the century. One of the worst weather disasters ever to hit North America, and the worst natural disaster ever recorded in Canada.

More than five million people lose power, some for more than a month. In Ontario, an estimated 11,000 hydro poles are smashed. The damage in Quebec is double that. More than 10,000 farms are affected in Ontario; more than 13 million litres of milk have to be dumped. Hundreds of cattle perish or have to be killed.

In Quebec, nearly 460 shelters accommodate people who have lost power and can't heat their homes. In Ontario, nearly 100 such shelters are established, the bulk of those to the east and south of Ottawa. Thousands of volunteers pitch in to help; millions of dollars in supplies—everything from food and blankets to generators—are either donated or loaned. The military does a magnificent job of rescuing people and animals, bringing in much-needed supplies, opening roads, and even assisting hydro crews in restoring power. In all, some 16,000 troops and reservists rush in to help. Hydro crews from as far away as Ohio, Manitoba and Saskatchewan respond to our cry for help.

Total damage is estimated at almost five and a half billion dollars. Three weeks after the storm moved on, 700,000 people were still without power. At the height of the storm, 57 communities in Ontario, including almost all from Kingston in the west, the Quebec border in the east and Ottawa to the north, declared a state of emergency. More than three million people lost power at least for 24 hours, half of those in Ontario. About 100,000 people spent at least one night in a shelter in Ontario and Quebec.

Sadly, 35 people died from causes directly related to the storm. House fires, falling ice and carbon monoxide poisoning are the major causes of death.

It's a terrible ordeal for thousands of people, but in some ways it's wonderful. Disasters of this nature often do bring out the very best in people, and certainly in Ottawa and the Valley, the best is very good indeed. Food, blankets, cots, diapers, even medical supplies, pour into the shelters. Police and the military drive and tramp over miles of dangerous roads to check on people and sometimes rescue them. Farmers share generators, water, machinery and grunt labour to help keep livestock alive. An unmilked dairy cow will quickly die a painful death.

It is one of CFRA's proudest moments; in fact, many people in the Valley even today will tell you that CFRA was their lifeline. And if the truth be known, for some it was, literally as well as figuratively.

When CFRA morning host Steve Madely and I get to work that Monday morning, January 5, we have only the barest inkling of what lies ahead. During that first day and even into the second, the City of Ottawa was not hit nearly as hard as many parts to the south and east of us. Neither Steve nor I have any difficulty in getting to work that Monday morning.

We, along with most others, figure it will be over in a few hours. During my show, I begin receiving a few phones calls from residents of the Navan and Kemptville areas complaining of very bad driving conditions, but it's not until my good friend the late Hal Anthony phones from Kemptville, mad as hell, that I begin to sense the gravity of the situation. "Come on, you guys," he says, "things may be fine in the big city, but I want to tell you that out here in the sticks, things are getting very bad. They're closing down some roads, some residents in Bishop's Mills and even here in Kemptville have lost power, this is bloody serious!" Not his exact words, but close enough. He is upset that the growing crisis in the rural areas is being ignored.

Steve Madely and I hold an emergency meeting and agree that from the information we are receiving, this storm is much more serious than we first suspected.

The decision is made to turn our entire radio station over to assisting victims of the storm in whatever way we can. We suspend all regular programming on CFRA and "Operation Ice Storm" is launched. All station personnel, including sales and technical staff, are pressed into service. Calls go out to schools of journalism for volunteers. A number of former employees rush to assist. A special switchboard is established with some operators working 16-hour shifts.

More than 26,000 phone calls pour in from Monday afternoon to Friday night. There are calls for help, offers of assistance, inquiries of every conceivable nature. We become a giant central clearing house. Calls for help are immediately transferred to the proper source—usually the military—that responds immediately. Offers of assistance are matched up with requests for various items and arrangements are made to have them transported to the appropriate location. If a call comes in for an item we don't have on our list, the request comes immediately to the newsroom where Steve Madely or I, or whoever is on air at the time, makes an appeal that is usually responded to within minutes.

The next morning, Tuesday, January 6, Steve and his support staff manage to get a station van down to Kemptville and begin broadcasting live from Grahame's Bakery, where the wood-fired oven is being used to cook food for dozens of people who have moved into a shelter at Kemptville College.

Kemptville, by Tuesday morning, is almost totally without power.

One of the great untold stories in all of this is the manner in which the late Ken Grahame, his son Rick and their entire staff at Grahame's Bakery kept their huge oven fired up for more than a week, in the end cooking food, I suspect, for more than half the town.

By the time Madely and his crew reach Kemptville, ice on some surfaces to the south and east of Ottawa is approaching an inch thick and getting thicker by the hour. Since telephones are out by this time, Steve's only means of communication is via a station van to which we have affixed a 30-foot-high makeshift aerial. This keeps coating up with ice, so during every break and newscast, Kiran Horra from CFRA's technical staff clambers onto the ice-coated roof of the van, pulls the aerial down, scrapes off the ice, and Steve is good to go for another 15 minutes. By this time, Steve himself is soaked through to the skin, but only recently confessed to me that the little airline-sized bottles of spiced rum that Ken Grahame kept stuffing into his pockets helped immeasurably!

At the conclusion of his show at 9:00 a.m., Steve and his crew manage to make it over treacherous roads to nearby Bishop's Mills where residents have been without power for almost 24 hours. As he begins describing on my show what he has experienced and what people are telling him about conditions, I begin to realize that we are facing a monumental disaster if someone in authority doesn't soon understand the gravity of the situation and begin to take action. Community leaders up until that point seem paralyzed.

As we begin to take more calls from desperate people, especially farmers, I take the bull by the horns and make a public cry for help from the military. I urge the mayors and reeves of cities and towns to appeal to the Province to declare a state of emergency and ask the military to bring in the troops. The call seems to galvanize officials throughout the Valley, including I might add, the Chair of Regional

Government in Ottawa, Bob Chiarelli, who begins to patch together a special task force, which does an excellent job in organizing assistance in the days that follow. It doesn't take the military long to respond either, because at one point in my broadcast, Steve Madely announces that Bishop's Mills is in desperate need of a stethoscope and syringes to assist some of the elderly people who had gathered at a shelter. Within the hour, a military truck pulls up at the shelter with two nurses, a medical kit and all the necessary supplies.

It wasn't until after the crisis was over, almost a week later, that General Rick Hillier, then Head of 2nd Mechanized Brigade, Canadian Forces Emergency Operations, tells me that his command post and all of his troops listened intently to CFRA 24 hours a day during the crisis, and immediately after we received a call from someone in need, they would rush to provide whatever assistance was required. "You were the lifeline," says General Hillier. "Quite frankly, we were listening to CFRA for the latest information and dispatching supplies and troops based on that."

Both Steve and I stay on the air all day for the entire week, taking requests for help from all over the Valley and, increasingly, from parts of Quebec. By the third day, things have grown even more desperate. Some of those calling are in tears. One farmer is sobbing; unable to milk all of his cows, he's had to slaughter some of them. Some dear friends call me during a break; they have been trucking water from the city to their farm near Ashton, but the horses are refusing to drink the strange-tasting water and they fear for their animals' lives.

There are times when I am reduced to tears by stories of people from all over the city rushing to the aid of those in need. School children are making cookies, even baking bread, and taking it to various shelters. Others who have power are taking in complete strangers and billeting them. At one point I receive a call from a shelter near Metcalfe. They have run out of potatoes. Within an hour, several hundred pounds of potatoes arrive. They pour in from all directions, along with hundreds of pounds of other types of food. On January 7, as I am driving in to work, I notice that many people in Kanata, which has not lost power, still have their Christmas lights burning. I suggest that maybe as a token show of support for the thousands who have had no power for two or three days, they might unplug the lights. Several residents phone the show to apologize, and the next morning I see that almost all the lights have been turned off. Little things sometimes mean a lot!

By this time Deborah and I have lost power at our home in West Carleton. After a night of darkness, cold, and no water, we move in with friends in Kanata. It's not safe to step outside at our house. Tree branches and sometimes entire trees are crashing to the ground. It's a sickening sound heard over thousands of acres, from Kingston almost to the east coast. Millions of trees are destroyed or so severely damaged they never recover. The maple syrup industry of Eastern Ontario and Western Quebec is severely crippled. Entire apple orchards are destroyed.

Even the gravest crisis is often not without its humour. Without water at our home, I was compelled to answer a call of nature beneath a giant pine tree that graces our backyard. I had no sooner unzipped than a huge branch came crashing down, forcing me to head for cover. My sister-in-law, who was staying with us at the time, was thus inspired to post a notice on our back door that read: "If you go outside to pee, don't do it under a tree!" Under the circumstances, excellent advice!

At CFRA, sometimes the calls for help would come in to Steve or to me from the person involved, but more often it was a friend or neighbour worried about someone they hadn't heard from in several days. Whatever the nature of the call, the military in a very admirable manner was able to respond almost immediately. Small wonder that today General Hillier is Chief of Defence Staff. He certainly displayed an amazing ability to size up a problem and solve it in record time. His organizational skills on display during this greatest of ice storms were nothing short of astonishing!

On January 7, three days into the storm, Steve and I conduct our entire morning broadcasts from a cavernous warehouse at CFB Uplands, where the military have assembled a huge supply of emergency items. Even as we broadcast live, with the freezing rain continuing to pour down, large trucks keep wheeling in, loading up and rolling out to various shelters with clothing, blankets, food, medical supplies, cots—and such other necessities as toilet paper and diapers, soap and bottled water.

But it wasn't just the military that was performing Herculean tasks. Keeping the CFRA lifeline on the air was becoming virtually impossible as the ice kept building on our broadcast towers. We lost electrical power first at our FM transmitter site atop Camp Fortune and then our AM transmitter near Manotick.

As you might expect, we have emergency generators at both locations; the problem was the generators had to be supplied with diesel fuel. Somehow our Chief Engineer, Harri Jones, managed to track down a small tanker truck which he was able to use to keep the fuel flowing to the Manotick site. The real problem was getting sufficient fuel to the top of Camp Fortune.

Braving very dangerous roads to the base of the Camp Fortune mountain with the tanker truck, Harri and veteran CHUM technician Kiran Horra then had to fill two small 44-gallon barrels with diesel fuel, using a small hand pump, strap the barrels to a toboggan, and then tow them to the top of the mountain behind a 1961 Bombardier J5 snowmobile. All of this in steady freezing rain, rendering not only the roads and mountainside dangerous, but every tree a possible death trap as well. Fallen trees and limbs had to be cleared away from the path, both on the way up the mountain at Camp Fortune and again on the way down.

The emergency generators were never designed for prolonged use, thus had only relatively small fuel tanks, so for almost three solid days Harri and Kiran had virtually no sleep, dashing back and forth supplying fuel to both the Manotick and Camp Fortune transmitter site generators. As far as I am concerned, Harri and Kiran are two of the unsung heroes of the storm. By the way, a big thank you to the military for helping us stay on the air. On Wednesday, that is the third day of the storm, metal skis were welded to a 300-gallon tank that the army pulled up the mountain to fill the CHUM and CBC-TV fuel tanks.

By the fourth day, January 8, keeping CFRA on the air was doubly important. CJAD Montreal, a major source of information for English-speaking Montrealers, went off the air when its transmitting towers succumbed to the weight of the ice and came crashing down. CFRA's signal can be picked up, not only in the western portions of Montreal, but is easily heard throughout the Eastern Townships of Quebec, which had been devastated. So each hour, we turned our radio station over to CJAD for several minutes as they attempted to provide a vital lifeline for their listeners. CJAD's Gord Sinclair did for his listeners what Steve and I were doing for ours. We had the advantage of more time and a microphone. Gord had use only of a telephone, but was able to provide an invaluable service.

By the fourth and fifth days, many Montrealers were calling us directly at CFRA for assistance and information. We also volunteered the use of our airwaves to CJSS Cornwall which had also gone off the air, and devised a special fundraiser in conjunction with the Red Cross. Harri also provided invaluable service to CHUM stations in Kingston and Brockville.

After the storm was over, melting temperatures presented a new and very dangerous problem. Huge chunks of ice began to fall from the transmission towers throughout the storm area. Fortunately CFRA's towers escaped serious damage, but a chunk of ice weighing several hundred pounds came crashing through the roof of the CFLY Kingston transmitter building, and our FM station in Brockville also suffered heavy damage from falling ice and went off the air. Harri managed to track down replacement equipment from as far away as Toronto, and in the case of Kingston actually risked his life helping to install a temporary transmitter tower atop an ice-coated 17-storey building.

For the entire duration of the storm and for several days after, CFRA's switchboard was manned 24 hours a day and kept constantly abreast of all the latest information concerning shelters, rescue phone numbers, supply requirements, and so on. During some periods of the day and night, three and sometimes four special operators were answering as many as 100 calls an hour. More than 26,000 calls poured into our switchboard during that week!

In its lead editorial, the *Ottawa Sun* said, "Newspapers weren't immediate; television couldn't do it without power. But for tens of thousands in Eastern Ontario, battery-operated radios and 580 CFRA had thrown them a lifeline through the ice!"

The Great Ice Storm of '98 was the worst nature has ever thrown at us, but in true Canadian fashion we beat it! We stuck together. We helped each other. We shared what we could. It was one of our finest hours—and radio at its best!

One of the interesting things about all of this is what it did to our listenership. Not at all what you might think! We received well over a thousand letters and emails of praise and thanks, along with citations and awards. The Government Whip, Don Boudria, a resident of Eastern Ontario, even told the House of Commons, "CFRA became a form of emergency measures to a community of more than a million people in need." Despite that and the magazine salutes, newspaper articles, tributes from the Ontario Premier, from General Rick Hillier and many others, our efforts actually cost us listeners.

For communities to the south and east of Ottawa, the Seaway Valley and to no small degree Western Quebec, CFRA became their lifeline, but many former listeners in the City of Ottawa quickly became bored with the plight of others and turned to other stations programming something other than disaster and calls for help.

For most in the City of Ottawa, the ice storm was a minor inconvenience. A few trees down, maybe a few hours without power, large numbers were glued to the radio, ready to assist in any way they could, but the fact is, many others had little interest in what was going on, and audiences for most music stations and the CBC actually got a boost as significant numbers of regular listeners to CFRA turned away from us. I'm not in any way complaining or laying blame anywhere. It's just a fact of life in the broadcast industry. Most of our regular listeners came back to us, thank heavens, when regular programming resumed, but I didn't know whether to laugh or scream when several callers and emailers complained bitterly that the only reason we did what we did was to boost ratings!

The General Almost Kills Himself

You would be hard pressed during the 1960s, '70s and '80s to find a better known or more popular figure in Ottawa and the Valley than Ken

"The General" Grant, morning man at CFRA in Ottawa. Extremely hard working, flamboyant, a terrific showman and genuinely funny, he marched two entire generations off to school with his famous "FOR-WARD HO!"

In great demand as a public speaker and emcee, The General found himself keeping very late hours at one function or another almost every night. Couple that with the fact that our baseball team, The Happy Blunderers, played one and sometimes two games a week in such far-flung places as Pembroke, Moose Creek or Morrisburg. With the obligatory "few beers" after the game, you've got one very busy man with not much time for things like sleep.

As a consequence, Ken learned to grab a wink or two whenever he could. I've been at dinner functions with him when close examination of his eyes behind the blue-tinted glasses he used to wear revealed that even though he was nodding in apparent agreement with what someone was saying, he was actually asleep.

As far as I know he never nodded off during newscasts or commercials on his show, although it wouldn't surprise me if his producer, Henry Lane, had to do the odd morning prod to get him started again. Ken was a consummate professional, so there was no way a listener would ever suspect that the guy making us laugh so much on the radio had rolled out of bed that morning with maybe only a couple of hours of sack time.

Being young and full of energy, Ken never even contemplated slowing down until one morning when he was shocked to learn he had almost killed himself!

It was a morning pretty much like most others. To bed late, up in the early darkness for the drive from his chalet-like house in the Gatineau Hills to CFRA on Isabella Street. Good show, lots of laughs, lots of energy. Great to be alive. Nice new four-by-four in the parking lot.

Wait a minute, what happened to the ski rack on top of the vehicle? And what the heck is all that mud stuck in the door jam? A little buzz of memory and worry fires some electrodes in his brain. This is very puzzling. Oh well, I'll head home, he thinks, and maybe play some golf.

And then he sees it! Just across the Macdonald-Cartier Bridge, on the Quebec side, jammed firmly into the grassy shoulder of the highway—his ski rack. Oh my God! It all comes back in a flash. He's driving to work that morning, falls asleep at the wheel and incredibly, really incredibly, his vehicle rolls completely over and comes back up onto its wheels. Only this time instead of heading south across the Macdonald-Cartier Bridge, his vehicle is heading westward into Hull. Instinctively, but obviously still in some kind of sleep state, he goes into Hull and takes the Portage Bridge across the river and into Ottawa.

When he tells me about it after, Ken says he doesn't remember actually rolling over, but does have a vague recollection of heading towards the Macdonald-Cartier Bridge, and then awakening to wonder how he got on the road leading into Hull. Only when he spotted his roof rack on the side of the road did it all come back to him.

It was after that that Ken began checking himself into bed a bit earlier!

The General Is Missing!

We've had a lovely day cruising the Thousand Islands. Ken "The General" Grant, Ernie Calcutt, Don Holtby, their wives and a few other friends. Pizza in Alexandria Bay, a few cool ones while sailing past Boldt Castle, more than a few laughs along the way. Bright sun, sparkling water, now an aboard-ship cocktail before we head out to a small island restaurant upstream a couple of miles. The restaurant is The General's favourite. "No one," he claims, "makes frogs' legs nearly as good."

One by one our crew members slip away into the cottage for a brief shower or a fresh layer of lipstick. Finally, with everyone back on board (or so we believe), we're ready to cast off for our island dinner when Gail suddenly realizes that husband Ken hasn't returned. "Hold on for a minute," she says, "I'll go get him."

Several minutes later she reappears with a strange look on her face. "I can't find him." She sounds worried.

Thinking he's just fallen asleep someplace, I jump off the boat and check the cottage bedrooms. No sign of him. This is very strange. Where the heck can he be? Our tiny island just upstream from the Ivy Lea Bridge is not much more than a flyspeck. An old cottage, a bit of a patio, a few small trees out back and that's it. No place to get lost for heaven's sake. A cat couldn't find a place in which to hide! By now we're all getting very worried. There's a mass exodus from the boat, and a massive General hunt is launched amidst growing fear he may have dozed off and toppled from the island into the fast-flowing St. Lawrence River.

I'm on my hands and knees peering into the dust bunnies beneath a bed when I hear a strange sound coming from a tiny closet in the corner of the bedroom.

I yank open the door and there he is. Jammed into the closet, his hands over his head clutching the metal rod from which clothes are supposed to hang. He's fast asleep.

"KEN," I shout, "WHAT IN THE HELL ARE YOU DOING?!" He mumbles something which sounds strangely like "having a shower."

Having had probably only two or three hours' sleep in the last couple of days, Ken has laid down on the bed, thinking he'd grab a few winks. Then somehow realizing he's supposed to have a shower and head out for dinner, he rouses himself, opens the door to the tiny closet, reaches up, feels the metal rod, believes it's the shower head, goes to turn it on and falls fast asleep again, the enclosed space preventing him from falling over!

We get him what we think is fully awake, load him aboard the boat and off we go. There's much laughter at the dinner table, and more than a little relief that disaster was averted, but when Ken awakes the next morning, some ten hours later, he refuses to believe that he wolfed down not one, but two full orders of his favourite frogs' legs the night before!

Confession Time

I don't believe for a moment that confession is good for the soul. I suspect that little doozy was cooked up by the Catholic Church looking to fill a few more of those little booths with the sliding panels. The only reason I'm confessing now is that the main protagonist is no longer with us and it's well past the statute of limitations. In other words, they can't arrest me now for smuggling into Canada the uniforms, pads and other equipment for the Ottawa Sooners Junior Football Team.

At least I don't think they can arrest me!

Now I want to set the record straight, since this story has never been made public before. I didn't intend to smuggle anything into Canada, let alone an entire football team's equipment. As a matter of fact, I didn't even know I was smuggling until it was too late and we had already broken the law and entered Canada with the contraband.

It's the morning after our night of searching for the missing General Grant. We take a vote and all decide to boat across the St. Lawrence to Alexandria Bay, New York, and their famous Pancake House. Actually it was Don Holtby who first broached the idea. At various times in his career, Holtby was CFRA's General Sales Manager, General Manager of the Ottawa Rough Riders, and General Manager of the Ottawa Sooners Junior Football Team. To be honest, I'm not sure what his role was at the time of our little pancake expedition, but obviously he still had a keen interest in the Sooners.

We had a wonderful breakfast, all the pancakes and sausage you could eat for $2.95 as I recall, and for some reason no one seemed to note the fact that Don had slipped away.

He was there at the dock, however, when we hauled ourselves aboard for the trip home. He didn't say anything to me until we were well in Canadian waters and a police boat was coming up the channel towards us.

"I guess I'd better tell you," he said, "the new uniforms, pads and equipment for the Sooners are in your front cabin down below!"

I was thunderstruck. "What the hell! Geez, Donny, if that police boat stops and searches us, we're all in the slammer for the rest of our lives and this boat's up for auction!"

Donny had a funny little laugh, usually accompanied by a deep drag on a cigarette and raised eyebrows. He tried all three on me, but not until the police boat was well past did I dare breathe again.

Unknown to any of us, Don had ordered a new set of uniforms and pads for the entire Sooners team from an American firm, had it shipped to a friend in Alexandria Bay, and while we were all stuffing down pancakes it was loaded aboard my boat.

According to Don, it saved him several thousand dollars and I really don't think he realized the jeopardy he had foisted on us all. I've often speculated on the headlines that would have appeared the next day if we'd been caught. Don't forget, at the time General Grant, Ernie Calcutt and Lowell Green dominated Ottawa airwaves, and all three of us were aboard that boat, which by the way was named *The Greenline*. If I'd been a newspaper editor at the time, I know what my headline would have read: "FROM THE BIG TIME TO THE BIG HOUSE!" Subhead: "Up the River Without a Brain!"

There, actually I do feel a bit better having confessed. Maybe the Catholics *are* right!

Mystery, Shame and Honour

They tell me that Bob Wood, Parliamentary Secretary for Veterans Affairs in the Jean Chrétien Liberal Government was a pretty decent guy. If that is true, he must have been red-faced with shame the day he met Arthur Lee. Had it been under normal circumstances it might not have been so bad—but that the meeting should have occurred at the premier screening of the movie *John McCrae's War: In Flanders Fields* must surely have been one of the more difficult days in Mr. Wood's political career.

That is, assuming he had a conscience.

What led up to the meeting and the screening of the film is one of the most shameful and hypocritical episodes in a political regime filled with shame and hypocrisy.

It began on October 21, 1997, when I learned that a set of military medals belonging to one of the world's most famous soldiers was going to be put up for auction and that his native land—Canada—was quite prepared to let them leave the country forever. I am talking, of course, about medals that once belonging to Colonel John McCrae, author of "In Flanders Fields," arguably the best-known and best-loved poem ever written.

I could not believe it. Nor could my listeners. To confirm the story, I contacted the office of Heritage Minister Sheila Copps. "Surely," I said, "Canada will not allow the McCrae medals to be sold out of the country. They are among the most significant historical artifacts we have."

I was given a pile of buffalo chips about how Ms. Copps was doing everything she could to keep the medals in Canada, but "no" a spokesperson admitted, "the Government of the day was not prepared to put up a single red cent for their purchase." In short, the Chrétien Government, which at the time, we now know, was pouring millions into the pockets of its friends in Quebec and elsewhere, couldn't find the anticipated $30,000 the medals were expected to sell for.

I was livid with anger and made no bones about it on the air. Some of the terms I used to describe Ms. Copps and her government probably should not have been broadcast, but I make no apology.

I'll never forget what happened. The very first caller, just as angry as I, said, "Lowell, if the damn government won't do anything to save these medals for Canada, then why don't we Green Beanies do it. I'm kicking in $200 right now!" It started a tidal wave of similar calls and pledges.

By the end of the program, we had $27,000 pledged with more rolling in by the minute.

Realizing the difficulty of keeping track of all of this, and aware that there are always people prepared to think the worst, we made arrangements for all money to be sent to the National War Museum, then on Sussex Drive. They were absolutely delighted. At the time, the government was drastically cutting their budget, so the museum had no extra money whatsoever to make a bid for the medals that they dearly wanted.

A museum spokesman told me the next day when I went to visit and make the arrangements that the McCrae Medals would certainly be one of their most prized exhibits and a major crowd attraction.

But hold it a minute. We have a problem! Even as more money flows into the War Museum, we are hit with a very strange mystery which may bring everything to a grinding halt.

On October 22, the second day of our campaign, the *Ottawa Sun* runs a major story claiming that Colonel McCrae's family, including Geills Turner, wife of former Prime Minister John Turner, and her brother, MP David Kilgour, don't believe the medals can be authentic. According to the *Sun*, the McCrae family believes the medals were lost at sea when a ship carrying McCrae's baggage was torpedoed and sunk. Family members say they will continue to investigate.

But, Dick Malott, former Curator of the War Museum, confirms to me that the medals are indeed real. "The medals," he tells me, "were sold by a distant relative to a private collector 30 years ago and this collector is now placing them up for sale."

Further investigation reveals that Mr. Malott is correct, although how this distant relative got the medals or who the relative was has never been made public. The McCrae family will only confirm that, yes, those medals are real. They really are the ones presented to Colonel McCrae.

Even though the Museum believes the medals will only fetch $30,000 at the auction, I decide not to take a chance. I have been privately informed that there is a well-heeled British collector who is very interested in the medals, along with at least two Americans and one person from Korea.

The idea that these medals could leave Canada forever, and even end up in Korea, drives my listeners crazy, and by the time the auction rolls around that Saturday, more than $80,000 has already been received with more pledged. We fully believe we have more than enough to buy the medals and keep them in Canada.

How foolish we were.

The bidding war for the medals is incredibly fierce. The Canadian government isn't the least bit interested in the medals, but many others are.

Our brave but in the end pitifully inadequate $80,000 is outbid in the first ten minutes of the auction. Museum officials are crushed and shamed. So am I.

Thank God there was at least one Canadian with enough pride and money to come to the rescue.

A Toronto garment manufacturer hardly anyone had ever heard of makes the final bid of $400,000 and immediately turns the medals over to the McCrae Museum in Guelph, the Colonel's hometown. The man who steps forward with pride, gratitude and $400,000 is Arthur Lee, who came to Canada in 1965. A humble man, Mr. Lee says simply, "I wanted to show my love and gratitude for my adopted country!"

One of the things I am most proud of is the fact that every single contributor to the McCrae Medals campaign was notified by the War Museum that if they wished, their donation would be returned in full to them, or it could be left with the museum to acquire other artifacts. Almost without exception, our donors left their money with the museum.

So now, just picture this... About a year later, on November 9, 1998, Bob Wood, representing the government that had no interest in Colonel McCrae's medals, is there on the podium with Arthur Lee, introducing a National Film Board documentary entitled *John McCrae's War: In Flanders Fields*.

Here are Mr. Wood's words on that day of supreme hypocrisy:

"Lt. Col. John McCrae was a true Canadian hero: a doctor, a soldier and poet. It is partly because of his haunting poem that we will never forget the extreme sacrifice made by our soldiers to safeguard our peace and freedom."

To which I can only add, yeah right! We won't forget, unless of course we have to yank a bit of money away from our political friends, in which case we simply will say, Colonel John *who*?

The film, which was shown on Remembrance Day 1998 by the CBC, probably cost far more than $400,000 to produce.

The McCrae medals are now a major attraction at the McCrae Museum in Guelph.

Lt. Col. John McCrae's gravesite is marked with a simple and sadly neglected inscribed slab of concrete in Wimereux Communal Cemetery along the coastal road near Boulogne, France. He died on January 8, 1918, of pneumonia exacerbated by the chlorine gas he had inhaled during earlier fighting.

While not a poet, Igor Kusyszyn, a professor at York University, a man who says he lost relatives in the Ukraine to both the Nazis and the Communists, has written a few lines which obviously come from the heart and speak for many of us. His poem, below, is entitled "Thanks to Arthur Lee."

Oh, Arthur Lee, Arthur Lee
Millions of Canadians
Owe their thanks to thee.
You saved Dr. McCrae's medals
With your generosity.
Plunking down four hundred grand
You saved them for your adopted land.

What a model citizen you are
Having come to us from, oh, so far.
Where was the Canadian establishment
On that October morning?
The medals were up for auction,
Everyone had fair warning.
Shame, shame, shame,
The blue bloods' patriotism went lame.
Let us all bend a knee to Mr. Lee,
His gift has preserved the memory
Of Canadians lying in Flanders Fields
Having bravely fought and died so far away
So that we may have the freedom we have today.

Return to Little Stalingrad

"**T**he damn stupid Limeys—it's a wonder they didn't get us all killed in Ortona, the bloody blockheads!" It was an oft-repeated theme from my stepfather and one of the last things he said to me before a high-voltage wire took his life in the fall of 1956. It still shakes me to think that this guy, Bert Whetter from Cannington, Ontario, fought his way with the Seaforth Highlanders, through the mud, the rain and the cold of Sicily, up the boot of Italy, through the deadly streets of Ortona, only to die as a lineman repairing hydro wires for the City of Brantford.

In fact, Bert was one of those Canadians who, when the heavy lifting was done in Italy, was shipped off to help liberate Holland.

More than two years fighting the best the Germans could throw at him without a scratch, only to have his luck run out atop a hydro pole in bucolic Ontario.

And, according to him, it was only luck that saved his life during the fierce, hand-to-hand fighting in Ortona. "We lost almost 1,500 men—killed, mind you, lots more wounded, some terribly in only about four days, and you know something?" he would tell anyone who would listen, "I blame the damn Brits! The Limey buggers!" Sometimes he used much harsher language, especially after a few beers.

His assertion was that during the prolonged training in Britain for the Italian campaign, their instructors insisted on following the British textbook method of close-quarter urban fighting. "The damn fools," said Bert, "told us the way to roust the Germans from buildings, especially houses, was to go door-to-door along the streets, enter the ground floor, clear every room up to the top, then do it all over again with the next house. Most of our men thought this was about as stupid a way to go about it that anyone would devise, but would any of the brass listen? Of course not! That's the way the bloody manual said it had to be done and that's the way we trained for weeks."

According to Bert, and historians agree, the Allies advanced through Sicily and southern Italy with relative ease. Aside from the mud, it was pretty easy going, according to most. Much of the opposition came from the Italian army that, from most reports, really had little stomach for the fighting. Bert often told me that many Italians greeted them as liberators rather than as conquerors. "Forget that bit about sunny Italy though," Bert would laugh, "there was nothing but mud, rain and cold. The only time I was really warm," he once told me, when my mother was nowhere near, "was when we 'liberated' a wine cellar." Pausing a moment, he added, "Actually, we were probably just as cold, but after a couple bottles of that wine, no one cared."

But the nature of the fighting began to change as the Allies approached Rome. To protect the ancient city, the Germans had established an elaborate line of defence all the way from Monte Cassino in the west, along the Moro River to the Adriatic Sea in the east. Pivotal for the Germans was the small Adriatic seaport town of Ortona that Hitler had ordered must be defended at all costs. "There can be no retreat from Ortona," ordered Hitler.

While the Americans and the British were ordered to attack what was called the Gustav Line in the west, anchored by Monte Cassino, the 1st Canadian Division, under the command of General Christopher Vokes, prepared to attack the eastern portion of the line whose main defences were in Ortona.

The Canadian advance toward Ortona began the night of December 5, 1943. Princess Patricia's Canadian Light Infantry crossed the Moro River under cover of darkness and captured the small village of Villa Rogatti. The Seaforth Highlanders, fighting fiercely, with young Bert Whetter in the ranks, managed to secure a bridgehead across the Moro near the town of San Leonardo. On December 8, the Canadians continued their assault, and on December 9, they drove the Wehrmacht from San Leonardo.

Now the Canadians were up against the very best soldiers the Germans had to offer, seasoned veterans of the 3rd Battalion of the 1st Parachute Division, entrenched in a long ravine just to the south of Ortona. Several days of terrible, sometimes hand-to-hand, combat ensued, but on December 13, the Canadians, led by the Seaforth Highlanders and the West Nova Scotia Regiment, broke through the German lines. On December 14, the Van Doos (the Royal 22nd Regiment) and the Royal Canadian Regiment suffered such heavy losses in desperate fighting that their effectiveness as a fighting unit was severely depleted.

By now the Allied press was referring to Ortona as a "second Stalingrad." It was an apt description since the battle for Ortona would become the bloodiest fight in the entire Italian campaign. House-to-house, hand-to-hand combat in Ortona began on December 21, with the Canadians taking terrible casualties, largely because of their inadequate training back in England.

The Germans, old hands at close-quarter urban fighting of this nature, knew exactly what to do and understood only too well what tactics the Canadians were likely to use. So they deployed troops on the upper floors of all the buildings lining the narrow streets, set mines in some of the houses and littered the streets with rubble.

Following the British textbook meant that the German defenders could shower grenades down on the Canadians as they entered the ground floors of the houses. Even worse, if the Canadians did manage to clear a house of the enemy, they had to exit the building and run a gauntlet of gunfire through the street to the next building. The streets and houses were death traps. All but one member of an entire platoon from the Loyal Edmonton Regiment were killed when they entered a mined house. The lone survivor was rescued after being trapped beneath rubble for 80 hours.

Bert Whetter was probably correct when he stated that had the Canadians continued to follow the British "textbook" method they would have been wiped out entirely.

Thank heavens it didn't take the wily Canadians long to figure out the proper method of attack. As in most old European towns, each building is attached to the next, so the Canadians simply invented what they called "mouse-holing." Punch a hole through a building, preferably at the top level, so they could drop grenades on the Germans below. It also meant they didn't have to enter the killing fields of the streets. The Canadians advanced down street after street in this manner, mouse-holing from one building to the next. When possible, they would clear both sides of the street at the same time.

On the evening of December 24, that is Christmas Eve, 1943, with about half of Ortona in Canadian hands, but with fierce fighting still underway, some Canadians troops began quietly withdrawing from their frontal positions to the relative safety of the basement of a bombed-out church where a special Christmas Eve dinner had been prepared. For those who survived it was a memorable event, so much so that—thanks to listeners of my show and readers of Earl McRae's column in the *Ottawa Sun*—55 years later a number of those men made a pilgrimage back to that same church for an historic Christmas Eve dinner with some of the Germans against whom they had fought so bitterly.

The idea of the pilgrimage was first presented to me by Peter Goldring, at that time a Reform Party MP from Edmonton North. "We're trying to organize a Christmas Eve dinner for Canadian and German veterans in Ortona to mark the 55th anniversary of that first Christmas Eve dinner," said Peter, "but the damn Liberals have no interest."

He went on to explain the significance of the first dinner and how some of those who were pulled out of the line on Christmas Eve in 1943 didn't survive the next day's fighting. "No doubt," said Peter, "for some of those men, that dinner was their last. I don't know if you are aware of this," Peter added, "but by the time the battle of Ortona was over and we had won, 1,375 young Canadians lay dead and more than 900 were wounded. That's more casualties than the combined British and Canadian forces took on D-Day."

To my astonishment, I subsequently learned that Canada suffered more casualties during the battle for Ortona than the Americans experienced during the D-Day assault of Omaha Beach, considered one of the bloodiest battles of WWII.

The terrible casualty list only served to reinforce my doubt about the proposed pilgrimage. "Do you really think the Canadian vets will be willing to forgo Christmas here at home to sit down with a bunch of Germans, against whom they fought? That was one of the fiercest battles of the war. It was hand-to-hand at times."

Peter assured me that, in fact, a number of veterans, both in Canada and in Germany, had already expressed great interest in the project. "Yes, there's no question the fighting was fierce," admitted Peter, "but you know something? Old soldiers have great respect for a brave and tenacious enemy and there's no question that the Germans fought very bravely."

The problem was that the Government had no interest whatsoever in helping to finance the trip. "What are we looking at here?" I asked.

Probably in the range of $100,000 to $150,000 was the figure I was given, depending upon how many Canadian vets wanted to take the trip. I was dubious that we could raise anything close to that amount, but agreed to take the idea to my listeners and see what they had to say.

The response staggered me. My listeners were fascinated with the idea. Many were only vaguely aware of the terrible battle for Ortona. Many others admitted total ignorance of the entire Italian campaign, but as some actual veterans and then historians began to call and explain what a difficult, heroic and vital feat we Canadians had accomplished, the money began to pour in. Earl McRae took up the cause in his column in the *Ottawa Sun*, as well, and within three days we had more than $200,000 pledged. One anonymous couple, in a magnificent gesture, insisted that they wanted to pay the full cost of airfare for all the vets. I subsequently learned their identity and we have become good friends.

By the time I began begging people to stop donating, we had in excess of $280,000 in the bank. It was nothing short of incredible. Some might say a kind of miracle.

Now began the political intrigue. The Liberals, sensing they were losing a public relations coup, began to sniff around to see if they might make some political hay. Pointing out to us that government assistance was required in order to deal with special travel arrangements, and in particular to establish contacts with German veterans, they sent us a special liaison officer who, to be kind, didn't exactly endear himself to any of us involved in the project. In fact, so unpopular did this little guy become that while in an Ortona pub, just prior to the anniversary dinner, he became embroiled in a dust-up with none other than Victoria Cross winner Smokey Smith, who called him a "little Hitler" and threatened to punch him out. Earl McRae had to intervene and avert what could have been a mighty nasty scene indeed. Earl has assured him that despite the fact Smokey was well into his eighties at the time, he would have "smoked" our officious little friend.

While the "liaison officer" and I didn't get into any kind of real scrap, verbal or otherwise, things did get mighty testy during one meeting when I threatened to return all the money thus far collected from my listeners if the Liberals didn't do the job they were supposed to.

The agreement was that Peter Goldring's office would recruit Canadian veterans who wished to go to Ortona and make all the travel arrangements for them, but it would be our government's responsibility to make the proper contacts with the German Government and thus guarantee that German veterans would, in fact, attend the dinner.

A group of about ten of us met frequently in the West Block on Parliament Hill to review progress and then later to discuss the possibility of erecting a monument to fallen Canadian soldiers in the Ortona town square with the excess money that had been donated. During one of these meetings, I learned that as yet no German veterans had been contacted. In other words, our "liaison officer" hadn't done his job.

I became very concerned and informed everyone present that I could not in good faith continue to support the project if, indeed, there was not a strong contingent of German veterans at the dinner. "If we don't have some of the German vets at that dinner," I said, "then I will have to go on the air and inform my listeners what was happening and why, and offer to return all the donated money! It will be very embarrassing for all of us!"

Without going into greater detail, let me just say that the phone lines to Germany began to hum!

And so it was that on Christmas Eve 1998, the veterans of two mighty armies, who as young men were locked in a life-and-death struggle with each other, shook hands, clapped each other's shoulders, sat down, and together ate, drank, laughed and cried. Fifty-five years later, at peace with themselves and each other.

Most of those who attended that wonderful anniversary dinner are gone now. Their numbers truly do dwindle down to a precious few. They will never be forgotten. Certainly not in Ortona, where a very moving monument honouring those brave young Canadian men who fought for the town now stands in the main square. It is fitting, I suppose, that the monument was conceived, designed, constructed, erected and paid for, not by government, but by a grateful public, in this case listeners to my show and readers of Earl McRae's newspaper column. It was one of my proudest moments. I know Earl feels the same way.

I heavily promoted and helped to organize the movement to wear red on Fridays, as a way of showing support for our troops. Above is a photo of the giant Wear Red Rally held on Friday, September 22, 2006. It was a sea of red on Parliament Hill!

Just prior to addressing the Wear Red Rally on Parliament Hill, I broadcast live to the audience of Calgary talk-show host Dave Rutherford.

ABOVE: Two roasters and a roastee! Two of my best friends, Rick Young (left) and Paul Niebergall just prior to my 50th anniversary roast (April 2006) attended by 850 people. More than $85,000 was raised for Food Aid that evening.

Photo reprinted with the express permission of: "Ottawa Citizen Group Inc.", a CanWest Partnership.

I welcome broadcasting legend Max Keeping to the 2007 Food Aid broadcast from the Central Experimental Farm. Money raised is used to buy cattle from local farmers. The meat is then donated to local food banks. By the way, I used to be Max's boss, way back when!

Just some of the awards presented to me for the highly successful Aid for Aiden campaign. More than $125,000 was raised. A life was saved.

Jean

There are days when the apathy of listeners and the banality of callers have me seriously considering jumping from tall buildings. There are other days when their concern, compassion and kindness reduce me to tears.

You may remember "Jean's" call. It was just before Christmas in 2006. Given the season, I was trying to keep the topic as light and cheerful as possible. Most callers seemed to be in an unusually upbeat mood. No whining, moaning or groaning. The complaints to management even slowed to a trickle! Then out of the blue came the call.

Her voice was strong and angry, but at times it slipped into something approaching tears.

"Why would they do this?" she asked. "We've never done anything to hurt anyone in our lives. Why would anyone want to hurt us?" It took me a minute to get the full story out of her.

She and her nearly blind husband had spent the day shopping for their grandchildren. "We're pensioners and we don't have a whole lot," she said, "but we always save up to buy our grandchildren some special presents for Christmas."

They piled the few presents into the trunk of their car, pulled it up into their driveway in one of the residential areas of Vanier, and then went to bed in happy anticipation of an early morning drive to their son's home outside the city.

During the night, punks not only broke into the trunk and stole all the presents, but managed to pretty well destroy the interior of the car as well. The dash was smashed, seats slashed, wires ripped from their moorings, and windows broken.

"We're devastated," says Jean. "We don't know what to do. We can't afford to replace the presents, let alone replace the car. Why would anyone do this?" she asks again. "We've been good neighbours." Her voice is now filled with anguish. "I don't know what we're going to do or how we can explain to our grandchildren that we don't have any presents for them. Why would people want to hurt an old woman and a blind man?" She pauses and speaks more softly. "We just buried my mother and I had to borrow money for the funeral. How can we get the car fixed, how will Jerry be able to get to his doctor's appointments?" You could not help but be moved as she fought tears.

There is no question in my mind that my listeners will respond immediately to any appeal I launch on Jean's behalf, but I have a problem.

"How much do you think it will cost to replace the presents and repair your car?" I ask. "I'm sure my listeners will want to help you."

She is shocked.

"Oh, Mr. Green," she says, "that's not why I called. I don't want money from anyone. Most people today have enough trouble buying their own presents at this time of year. All I want is for the police to catch those people who did this to us and make them give us our presents back. Probably somebody saw those people smashing our car; if they would just come forward now and call the police, maybe we could at least get our presents back. That's really all I want."

She adamantly refuses to allow us to use her last name and insists that she will not accept any money from anyone. She keeps repeating, "That's not why I called."

Feeling helpless, I have to let her go. My lines immediately are jammed. The first caller is angry with me. "Lowell," he says, "you've got to get her last name so we can send some money and help her out. You just can't let this go." The next caller is one of Jean's neighbours. "I know her and her husband, Jerry," she said. "They're both salt of the earth. We had an apartment fire here not long ago, and Jean and Jerry were out there with blankets and hot coffee helping the people who had been evacuated. A couple of them even spent the night in their house, I think. Jerry can barely see, but he was doing everything he could do to help too. A lovely couple. This should not have happened to them."

Thinking quickly, my producer Ronnie Roberts obtains Jean's phone number and calls her back, not once, but three times, each time begging her to let our listeners help. "As you can hear," she tells Jean, "people really want to help you and your husband. Please let them."

But Jean continues to insist that she won't accept any help other than helping police catch the punks who smashed her car and stole the presents.

Despite this, cash donations begin to flood into the station. People double-park their cars on George Street, dash in and drop off loonies, toonies and bills of all denominations, including several $100 bills. One woman phones to say her son has just emptied his piggy bank and insists on leaving the pile of quarters, nickels and dimes at our switchboard. Others call to offer to pay the deductible on her insurance so the couple can afford to repair their car. Offers of presents pour in, and in fact, several presents, including teddy bears and dolls, are dropped off at our switchboard.

By next morning, close to $2,000 in coins and bills is piled up in a cardboard box our receptionist has used as a temporary bank. Ronnie calls Jean again, and once again attempts to persuade her to accept the money. Finally, somewhat less emotional than on the previous day, Jean agrees, but insists that she will only take sufficient money to get the car running again and replace the presents. "Look," says Ronnie, "use some of the money to rent a car so you can get to your son's place for Christmas. Your car won't be repaired by then." Reluctantly, Jean agrees.

Because of the publicity, I decide against presenting the money to her at her home. That might be just inviting more trouble, so Jean arranges to meet me the next day at her bank where she can immediately deposit the cash into her account.

When I arrive at her bank on Montreal Road shortly after my show on December 22, with a box filled with cash, and an armful of assorted teddy bears and dolls, Jean rushes to meet me, throws her arms around me and begins to cry. There are tears in Jerry's eyes as he reaches out to shake my hand. Some of the people in the bank must have heard our broadcasts and quickly realize what is going on because several break into applause. I, of course, begin to blubber, and as word flashes around the bank what is happening, there isn't a dry eye in the place!

"Merry Christmas, Mr. Green," says a smiling teller as I leave.

Yes, indeed!

Aid for Aiden

On September 23, 2003, Frank Cirella, President of the Pembroke Petawawa Lions Club received the following letter:

Dear Mr. Cirella,

I am writing this letter to request your help and support in raising money for the family of Aiden Russelle. Aiden was born on October 29, 2001 with life-threatening complications stemming from a rare congenital disorder where his liver and some of his intestines were outside of his stomach. Associated with this disorder was a very serious heart problem; a hole in his heart and one of the main heart valves which normally pumps oxygenated blood throughout the body was destroyed. To assist you in understanding Aiden's medical history (he has undergone 15 surgeries so far), I have included a description of some of the complications Aiden has faced.

We are extremely fortunate to live in Canada, where all care provided by a physician or in a hospital is paid for under Medicare. However, Aiden requires a great deal of care when he is at home too. Since his birth, the cost of his nursing care, medical equipment, and transportation to the Children's Hospital of Eastern Ontario has cost the Russelle family their life savings. Aiden has spent two-thirds of his life at CHEO, undergoing various surgeries and recovering from recurring infections that are caused by the tracheotomy which helps him breathe. Kelly, Aiden's mom, has not been able to return to her job as a teacher, since Aiden requires full-time care. Stuart, a Corporal here at 2 Field Ambulance, has received as much financial support as his co-workers can muster on their own, but it is simply not enough. A breakdown of medical expenses incurred in the past two years is enclosed after this letter.

In addition to the ongoing medical costs the Russelle family has already paid, Aiden needs another major surgery to remove the tracheotomy and repair the damage it caused. This surgery should be the last big procedure until Aiden gets to be five or six years of age, when he will require another open-heart operation. If all goes well with this surgery, Aiden will be able to eat normally and talk for the first time in his life. Unfortunately, this surgery is extremely complex and is not performed in Canada, so the Russelles must travel to Cincinnati, Ohio this spring. A breakdown of the anticipated costs (travel, meals, etc.) is enclosed.

We have done our best at 2 Field Ambulance to help with the costs of Aiden's care, but we wish to do more. Although we do not have the fundraising experience of a service club such as your own, we are very committed and passionate about helping the Russelle family pay for the necessary medical expenses to help Aiden. The Russelle family has already received very generous support from the community, as detailed in the enclosed table, but the surgery in Cincinnati will require a dedicated fundraising campaign. It is our hope that you will consider helping us in this endeavour. We have several ideas about how to proceed; however, any expertise you might lend would be very much appreciated.

Please feel free to contact one of the leaders of our Aiden Russelle Fundraising Team [here Colonel Grondin lists the names of several people and their phone numbers which for privacy purposes I have deleted]. Although I have no doubt you receive countless requests for support, I sincerely hope you might find a way to help us make the costs for the Russelle family a bit easier to bear. Aiden has been so brave throughout his many surgeries and treatment and we simply wish to help his family focus on his future, rather than his medical expenses.

Thank you for your consideration.

Sincerely yours,
[signed] J. Grondin, Lieutenant-Colonel
Commanding Officer, 2 Field Ambulance
Canadian Forces Base, Petawawa

Brief Summary of Aiden's Medical History
- Aiden was born with a rare congenital disorder on Oct 29, 2001 and immediately rushed to CHEO.
- His intestines and liver were on the outside of his stomach;

associated with this condition was a serious heart defect.

- The original goal of the medical team was to push his liver and intestines back in and then repair his heart. To do this, they had to put a tube into his throat. This damaged his vocal chords and the trachea (windpipe), resulting in a lot of scarring, so they had to put in a neck tube or tracheotomy to enable Aiden to breathe.

- To meet the first goal of getting his organs where they belonged, it took three surgeries—one to push everything in, one to fold the skin over his abdomen and one to close the muscle.

- The heart problems were the next concern, and were addressed in the same timeframe as the later surgeries to correct the liver and intestine problems. Aiden had two holes in his heart, a hole between the ventricles, one valve was destroyed, and one ventricle got too big and was crowding out the other. These problems meant that without corrective open-heart surgery, Aiden would be blue because the mixture of oxygenated and non-oxygenated blood in his body would not be correct.

- To keep Aiden pink, while waiting to be able to finish the stomach surgeries, two shunts were put in his heart. These open-heart surgeries were performed on Dec 23 and Dec 24, 2001.

- Another open-heart surgery was needed when Aiden was one (last October) to repair the heart—major complications resulted in a three-month stay.

- Right now, Aiden has a heart the size of an 11-year-old child, which causes his one lung to have problems performing properly since his heart is crowding it out.

- An aneurysm developed out of this surgery and was repaired on 24 Mar 03 (another open-heart surgery).

- To complete the repairs to his heart, Aiden will need two more heart surgeries—a new valve at the age of five or six, and one more when his heart is fully grown—around age 14.

- Associated with these surgeries have been several heart catheterizations (take picture of heart by inserting catheter through leg) in preparation for the open-heart surgeries.

- All this medical treatment resulted in a great deal of damage to Aiden's windpipe, to the point that he now has a tube in his throat (called a tracheotomy), which effectively acts as his mouth. Aiden has had throat surgery already to try to remove the scar tissue, but the surgery was ineffective.

- Since Aiden breathes through the tube in his throat, he cannot eat with his mouth.

- Yet another surgery attached a "J" tube to bypass his stomach; this means Aiden is fed directly into the small intestine. This also means Aiden needs to be fed with a pump for 18 hours each day.

- This tube has had to be replaced several times, resulting in more trips to CHEO with complicated procedures.

- In total, Aiden has had 15 major surgeries in his 21 months, four of which have been open-heart surgeries.

- All the while, he has had to battle infectious disease. His tracheotomy tube makes him very susceptible to infection since there are only three cms of tube between his lungs and the open air.

- Aiden has had many respiratory illnesses, three of which were pneumonia caught in CHEO during hospital stays (one with a 35–50% mortality rate which he survived twice!)

- To fix the problem with his windpipe, Aiden needs two more surgeries—one is scheduled for 30 Oct 03 and will result in a minimum 14-day stay at CHEO. If this surgery is in fact needed (tests are not complete yet), his medical team would put the tube into his stomach instead of his intestine.

- Dr. Cotton, the world's leading expert in pediatric airway surgery in Cincinnati Ohio, will decide when the next surgery is; the Russelles will find out in the next two weeks. It will be around Jan–Apr 04. After the surgery, Aiden will need to be completely sedated for 2–3 weeks to ensure he doesn't move at all, plus 2–3 weeks to be weaned off all the sedatives.

- Dr. Cotton estimates it will take a 30–40 day stay at the hospital in Ohio if there are no complications. Dr. Cotton has said this is a very optimistic estimate.

Aiden's Daily Care

Aiden's parents, Stuart and Kelly, needed special education to be able to have Aiden at home. Among other things, they had to take an eight-week course in tracheotomy care.

- Everyday the stomas (holes where the tubes go into Aiden's body) need to be cleaned, and the tubes need care and changes —this takes about 45–60 minutes each day.

- Aiden needs suctioning every half-hour to keep his airway clear.

- He is given medication through the tube 4–5 times a day.

- He needs to be monitored *constantly* to ensure there are no obstructions in his tube, and he often needs a humidifier and oxygen when he sleeps.

- The Russelles must have nursing staff present from 2300–0700 everyday, as well as any time they need a break to take care of errands, or to take their six-year-old son, Joshua, on an activity outside the home.

- Aiden averages 1–2 times a week in CHEO. Kelly brings a

nurse or health care aide with her as she cannot make the trip with Aiden alone.

- Aiden sees an occupational therapist once a week, same with a physiotherapist, infant development worker and speech therapist (working on tongue movements and swallowing exercises since Aiden has never been able to eat with his mouth).

- Now that Aiden is able to balance a bit better, Kelly can occasionally take him with her to run errands such as grocery shopping. Each time Aiden goes outside the home, he needs a portable suction machine with sterile water, an emergency bag with breathing bags and extra medical supplies, a diaper bag, the feeding pump, and a big stroller to carry it all!

Aiden's Future

Aiden is now 23 months old and his prognosis is great. Two months ago he was assessed by infant development at CHEO and they expected him to be at 5 months of development and he's at 13 months development—he's a fighter! They expected severe developmental delays or retardation, but Aiden has not experienced this. There is nothing wrong with him that can't be fixed with "new parts." Once these issues are solved he will be at the low end of normal (running and playing) physically and normal in every other way. There is a light at the end of the tunnel for Aiden—Cincinnati is his last big step towards a more normal childhood.

Aiden's Expenses
One-time purchases

Item	Expense (approximate)
Heart monitor	$ 4,000
2 x Humidifier compressors	$1,600

Portable and stand alone suction machines	$1,400
Nebulizer (medication dispenser)	$250
3 x Bag valve masks	$720
Stethoscopes	$130
Custom made tracheotomy tubes	$1,800
Video baby monitoring system	$350
Cargo stroller	$500
IV pole	$75
Feeding pump	$1,600
Portable backpack for pump	$250
Special car seat to keep Aiden lying down	$1,000
Medical equipment stands	$100
2 x Air conditioners	$1,200
Miscellaneous equipment	$1,000
TOTAL:	*$16,000*

In order to give something back to the community, the Russelle family donates all medical equipment to others once Aiden has outgrown it or no longer needs it.

Routine purchases

The Russelles' insurance covers about 80% of most costs. The costs below are *after* their insurance has already paid the suppliers.

Item	Expense (approximate) per month
Cleaning and tracheotomy supplies	$65-$200
Night nursing care	$400
Avg. five trips to CHEO a month (in the past has included a nurse or attendant, gas, van rental as a car is too small for all	

the equipment, meals, and possibly overnight
at Ronald McDonald House) $750-$2,000

Specialized food for the pump $400

Oxygen (not always needed, and now on a plan) $500

Communications with CHEO (cell phone) $250

Special vaccines $50

Increases to hydro bill (need electricity on
all the time, also need to wash items around
Aiden several times, often with special
solutions and soaps) Varies

Increases to gas bill (need heat on all the time) Varies

AVERAGE TOTAL/MONTH: *$2,400 – $3,800*

In 2002, the Russelle family spent $36,900 solely on medical expenses. Kelly has been unable to return to work since Aiden's birth. Stuart only makes $35,800 after taxes.

Support Received for Aiden's Care

Thankfully, the Russelle family has not had to bear all the above expenses alone. They have had very generous support from the local community. The chart below lists the support provided since Aiden's birth.

Organization	Amount Received
Military Community	
(2 Fd Amb, 2 RCHA, CFMSS, Base)	$6,000
Support Association (Lions, Rotary, etc.)	$5,000
SISIP emergency grant	$5,000
Personal fundraising (family and friends)	$3,000
Miscellaneous	$2,000
TOTAL:	*$21,000*

In addition to the above, the Russelle family has had Joshua's daycare subsidized (i.e. fees were waived), Kelly's former workplace has been assisting with the Ronald McDonald house bills, a loan at 0% interest has been arranged, and a personal donation of GM points towards the purchase of a reliable vehicle has been made.

Future Expenses—Cincinnati

Stuart has completed a rough estimate of the costs associated with Aiden's surgery in Cincinnati, after consulting with the parents of Braeden Barker, another local child who faced overwhelming odds and medical expenses. Although the surgery is paid for, flights, accommodations, rental car, gas, meals, daycare for Joshua and incidental medical supplies will all need to be paid for (hopefully with the help of additional fundraising).

Stuart has estimated hotel expenses of $59 USD/night plus tax for the first 14 days, as Ronald McDonald House in Cincinnati has told him they do not accept pre-bookings and that he should expect a two-week waiting list. Once at Ronald McDonald house, the cost will be $15 USD/night.

Stuart has further estimated costs for meals, gas, flights, rental car, daycare and possible medical supplies (incidentals) for a total of 50 days, based on their extensive experience in Ottawa at CHEO. With possible donations of air miles for the flights, this estimate could be too high, although if Aiden has any complications, the estimate will be too low. Stuart estimates the total cost for the trip to be *$27,000* (Canadian funds). They will know soon exactly when the surgery will take place. For now, all they know is that it will most likely be between January and April, 2004.

[signed] J. Grondin, Lieutenant-Colonel
Commanding Officer
2 Field Ambulance

You can just imagine how Frank Cirella felt when he received that letter, especially knowing full well that it would be impossible for his organization to raise the required $27,000. "Just imagine how many car washes, bingos and raffles we would have to hold to get even close to that sum," he explained to me. "Besides which, we all knew that if Aiden was going to pull through, it would take years of medical care and many thousands more dollars."

He admits it was out of "pure desperation" that he summarized Colonel Grondin's letter, packaged it up with a picture of a grinning, chubby-cheeked Aiden Russelle, and fired it off to me at CFRA.

I receive dozens of appeals and requests every week, many of them very deserving. I must confess it sometimes breaks my heart to say no to them, but every once in a while there is a need so great, so obvious, that I know my listeners would be angry if I did not bring it to their attention and provide them the opportunity of helping.

As I progressed through my morning routine preparing for my show, I tried to put Frank Cirella's letter aside, but the picture of that happy little kid who was going through hell kept staring up at me. Try as I might, I just could not say no to Aiden Russelle.

To confirm that this wasn't someone's idea of a sick joke or a con, I phoned Frank Cirella at his Petawawa home. Got him out of bed, in fact!

"Frank," I recall saying, "what happens if the Russelles don't get the money to take Aiden to Cincinnati?" There was a long pause. "Well," he said quietly, "we will likely lose him."

"What about the parents?" I asked. "If we can't raise $27,000, are they the type likely to try to sue or raise hell in the media? What kind of people are they? Can I work with them?" Frank's reply was immediate and enthusiastic. "These people, Lowell, are the salt of the earth. You could not find better, more hard-working, more caring people if you searched the world!"

"It's Friday," I told him. "Leave this with me for the weekend. Let me think about it. It's a lot of money. I don't want to raise any false hopes here."

But I couldn't leave it for the weekend. I couldn't leave it for a day! That little kid in the photograph kept grinning up at me. Half an hour later, I was back on the phone to Frank. "I'm going to launch an appeal this morning," I said. "Forget the weekend. Where are the parents now? Do you know?"

"Geez, Lowell, I think they're in intensive care at CHEO right now. Aiden is in surgery again, I'm going to let the hospital know what's going on and maybe they can tell Kelly and Stuart."

In his 2004 presentation to the Canadian Association of Broadcasters Awards Committee, CFRA News Director Steve Winogron wrote: "Uncharacteristic of Ottawa's crusty broadcast veteran, Lowell Green actually broke down on the air and appealed to the compassion of his listeners to help little Aiden."

And it's true. As I explained to my listeners how this tough little soldier had undergone almost one major surgery for every month of his life, how he had never tasted food, not even his mother's milk, how he had never been able to utter a sound, I kept looking at that picture and I just couldn't hold it together.

The phone call from Aiden's parents calling in wonderment from CHEO is one of the most poignant moments in my life. An incredulous Kelly Russelle said: "We're in the ICU and listening, right now, to the radio program, and it's just amazing. It just warms our hearts." She was in tears. "You're gripping people by the heart," said

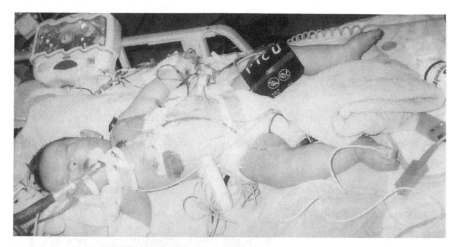

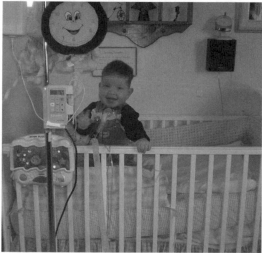

These are the pictures I had in front of me as I launched the "Aid for Aiden" appeal, which netted more than $125,000 and probably saved the little boy's life. I just couldn't say no to Aiden—and neither could many of you.

Stuart. "No," I replied, "it's Aiden who is gripping people by the heart!"

And as the phone calls and pledges poured in, I doubt if I was the only one having difficulty maintaining dry eyes. Our goal was $27,000, but three hours later when I signed off the show, the total pledged had ballooned past $40,000. But it didn't stop there. Monday morning's mail delivered armfuls of letters, almost all containing cheques. Some donors included pictures of their own children or grandchildren. Many included letters of encouragement and prayers for little Aiden. Cheques—by the thousands—continued to pour into CFRA for more than a week until Frank Cirella and the Pembroke Petawawa Lions Club was handed a cheque for more than $126,000. At their request, an overwhelmed Stuart and Kelly Russelle came on my show a few days later to issue a heartfelt thank you to everyone. There weren't many dry eyes around that day either!

The money was placed by the Lions Club into a special trust fund to pay for all of Aiden's medical costs not covered by OHIP. It literally saved the little boy's life. When he took that trip to Cincinnati, doctors were shocked to discover Aiden was suffering from a severe lung infection that would have taken his life within a few days. That crisis successfully dealt with, a decision was then made to delay for several years an attempt to remove the scar tissue in Aiden's trachea which prevents him from speaking and eating.

Aiden has undergone several more major surgeries since then, and while he has grown into an active, bright, robust young boy, he still cannot speak or eat. But there is hope that very shortly those Cincinnati doctors who saved his life will be able to perform the miracle that will enable him to fulfill his mother's most fervent wish: to hear him say "mommy." [As we were going to press with this book, we received wonderful news that the tracheotomy tube had been taken out of Aiden's throat and that he was doing well. This is a major step in Aiden's progress.]

Several months following the Aid for Aiden broadcast, I was the guest of the Pembroke Petawawa Lions Club and received a number of awards. Aiden was there and so were his parents, Stuart and Kelly. The picture of a happy little chubby-cheeked boy they presented to me—the one that once stared up at me from my desk—now hangs from my office wall.

It is my proudest possession!

What I Believe

We will get more of that which is rewarded.
We will get less of that which is punished.
> Columnist and broadcaster John Robson
> on CFRA's "Madely in the Morning," August 2007

The *Ottawa Citizen* once asked me what I thought was the key to success and longevity as a broadcaster. Conviction, I said. Conviction and a passionate belief in yourself.

There is a great deal more, of course. Hard work is certainly a good part of it. A thorough understanding of your community and your listenership, and an intense curiosity, are necessary in my business. But in the end, it is your core beliefs and your ability to understand and enunciate them that are the main deciding factors in how successful a public figure will be.

You must stand for something important and you must stand firm.

None of the following will come as any great surprise to those of you who listen frequently to what I have been saying for years, but since this is my last opportunity to spell it out in print, here for the record are some of my core beliefs, which I know I share with many of you.

Here is what I believe:

I believe socialism—the welfare state—goes far beyond forcing some of our most cherished institutions into near financial bankruptcy (e.g. health care), it has just about bankrupted us morally, as well.

I believe that the answer to most of the problems facing our country stare us in the face every morning when we look in the mirror, if we would just ask ourselves the right questions: What is important to me? What are my beliefs? Do things like virtue, morality, honesty and integrity mean anything to me? Forget the other guy, does honour mean anything to me? What about the work ethic?

I believe if we are to save the kind of civilization most of us cherish, we must relearn some very basic facts. To begin with, we must believe in the individual and the individual must believe in himself. We must accept less government in order to allow that individual maximum freedom to create and achieve. We must revisit our history lessons and rediscover that which is obvious: Societies founded on restraining government rather than restraining the individual are the only ones that can thrive. We must understand that the individual is almost always smart enough to solve his own problems and does not need to depend on big government for the resolution of all of life's difficulties.

I believe we must understand that the best we can hope for in a very imperfect world will most likely be achieved by maximizing individual economic and political freedoms and not through social utopian concepts and redistribution of wealth. We must also understand that at the core of a productive, prosperous civilization are strong wholesome family values that cannot be instilled by government edict, but can be sucked dry by well-intentioned but destructive government programs. Programs, for example, that provide free breakfasts for children in our schools, thus allowing irresponsible parents to avoid one more responsibility.

I believe that if the poverty industry, the socialists, the radical feminists, and other such left-wing groups which depend upon the creation of various crises to justify their existence, are really concerned about feeding children and eradicating poverty, they would be busily instilling in all those in difficult circumstances the kind of spirit that enabled tens of thousands of immigrants who came to this country and who still come, to pull themselves up out of poverty in just one generation or less. Too simplistic, you say? Look around you. How is it that immigrants, who came to this country a few years ago, often without a single cent in their pocket, unable to speak a word of English or French, are today the owners of countless businesses, or otherwise doing very well?

They are, for the most part, productive contributing citizens while we have countless Canadian-born people whose families have been on welfare or some form of government assistance for generations. Did going on the dole help these families? Or is it hard work, sacrifice and risk that make the difference? Look around you. The answer is everywhere you look.

I believe that we should do everything as a society to provide equal opportunity for everyone. That, however, does not mean we will all end up equal. The American constitution says all Americans are entitled to pursue happiness, it doesn't say anything about achieving it or guaranteeing it.

Our society should act as a launching pad. We should do everything we can to ensure we have an equal amount of rocket fuel for the launch, but after that, it's pretty well up to the individual. Few of us will make it to the moon. Some won't make it to Carp!

One of the sad aspects of our social policies is that only too often those who are really deserving of our assistance (and there are many) find there is nothing, or very little, left after the hordes of the non-deserving have gorged at the trough!

What we have done, and continue to do, is tell the individual they are helpless against the evil forces of capitalism, when the truth is, it is capitalism which provides the individual the best opportunity of achieving independence, financial and otherwise.

• • •

And this I also believe. All it takes to lose everything our forebears and we have worked and fought so hard for is just one generation of people who don't involve themselves in civics. One generation that cares nothing about their community or their country.

It will take only one generation of people who don't care or don't believe they have any responsibility for what occurs around them to lose much—or even all—of what so many of us hold dear. It's happened in other countries! The millions who attended the 1984 Winter Olympics in Sarajevo never dreamed that only eight years later, a vicious war would break out in those streets, killing more than 12,000 and virtually destroying that beautiful, modern city.

I believe it is time we—you and I—not the government—not a social worker—not the guy down the street—you and I do everything we can to ensure that no generation of Canadians be allowed to abandon their responsibilities to their families, to their community, to their country.

Which means that as long as I believe I'm helping some people get the message, I've got a responsibility to keep going. Problem is, the spirit may be willing, but the body is beginning to creak!

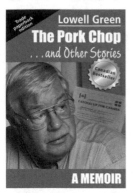